LIVE THE LIFE OF EMPOWERMENT

LIVE THE LIFE OF EMPOWERMENT

Find the *Light* within yourself
and live to free all that you are

Kefah Bates

To
The Beloved One

ISBN 978-1-9832046-0-9

Design by Ana Clara Bárbara & Kefah Bates

Cover image by Ana Clara Bárbara
after original by Eliska Vokounova

Contents

Introduction

I had to know the depth of struggle inside of me. It was hard to try to escape it, I was born into the world with pain and all those around me carried it too. No matter how much I would try to distract myself and live a 'normal' life I was always brought back to how much it hurt in my soul. I carried it in myself and for others it was something I could not help but do. I knew what the collective wanted from me, to succeed, gain and accumulate to bring happiness. I tried to know this life with all its traps but no matter how successful I was, in my heart I continually returned to the pain in me. I had no choice but to place myself in the path of all my deepest fears. I came to know suffering in myself and others with a relentlessness that would help me break every illusion to try to understand it. This drive came from the depths of me, a yearning within that believed in a much greater potential even if I didn't know what that was. Only afterwards did I realise what this drive meant and this was for inner peace and freedom from suffering.

When realisation comes there are no fireworks, parade or grand celebration; it comes with a knowing that this is truth, it was always there but is hidden behind intense discord. I wrote this book when peace was becoming, I learnt of universal truths that belonged to not just me but to all. I saw that empowerment came with no force, aggression or fight and is the realisation of our true state of being. To know the Holy is to know the self. I understood that to live empowered began by opening to a super sensitivity within and to have the courage to know all these shades. The movement to oneness is when the fire of our higher potential is lit and through this a world of endless possibilities waits.

I have come to know pain intimately, to understand its call and to see through it. The teachings of this book came through the research and transformations that occurred during my work as a healer helping others to understand their self and to transform their pain. The numbered paragraphs in each chapter are spiritual teachings, followed by guidance to help you integrate higher meaning into your life. They can be incorporated as daily meditations, prayers or for inner practice. It may resonate with you at different times of your life and ultimately help you. When you are looking for clear guidance or need to hear a voice that believes in you, then you can open the pages of this book and be reminded that you are not lost for all understanding lies within you. The intention of these higher truths is to help you believe in your ability to access your true power, for in your hands is the will to deliver into life the light that you are.

Kefah Bates
Edinburgh, Scotland
July 2018

I

YOUR TRUTH

LOSING TRUST IN YOURSELF

UNDERSTAND
for empowerment, you must trust yourself

LEARN
to place trust in all that is in you

BELIEVE
that you are not lost for you light the way

1.

Life is created from your own hands and this comes from truth.

Light exists in the knowing of what is real in you; this is the oneness of being. Without self-belief there can be no trust and reality becomes created out of fear. When you lose belief you will search for it outside of you. Light exists when you follow truth. Truth cannot be when you follow another. Life is created from your own hands and this comes from truth. What is created in the self exists because you have allowed it to be there. All that you are creates the life you lead, and all that you have become is being lived outside of your true shining. When you try to escape what you see within then trust in yourself is lost. Without self-belief the ability to make choices from truth is greatly weakened and so you will look elsewhere for guidance. By freeing light you return to the oneness of being.

GUIDANCE   The power of this teaching guides you to remember to pause and listen to what you feel about the experiences you have. In the rush of life you forget and only live a small potential of yourself. You get lost in the many constructs of what you think you should be doing. When you have strength to slow down, have the conviction to say 'above all the influences around me, in this moment I place aside what I know as right and wrong and open myself to what I really feel.' Listen to yourself and the response you are having from within. This is the start to growing truth.

2.

In true being you are incorruptible for here the Holy derives.

To be in light is the higher purpose to life. Because light is truth, you experience the integrated self. When in wholeness you create out of light and so live through a higher way of being. In the fall you forgot how to free the light within you and so it has become replaced with the illusion of pain. The loss of power comes through the separation from the oneness state within. In true being you are incorruptible for here the Holy derives. Treason within comes out of the battle to escape fear. Where there lies treason then trust cannot exist. You cannot blame another for what you have become but to believe in the truth of what you are. To live out of the inner fire comes when you master light within and cast truth, for all that lies in this higher potential is delivered through its wish.

GUIDANCE   I see how rare it is for people to truly believe that they possess all the answers within them. When you look outside for answers you do this out of fear of judgement from others. You place the opinion of another higher than truth. You become distracted by how others see you and fear standing apart. The Holy within you accepts all and knows no judgement. Turning away from what lies within fuels the reality of comparison, feeling of guilt and shame. Returning to inner knowing frees you from the fear of being true to yourself.

3.

Living light is to turn attention inwards and to follow this truth.

Potential lies within how you understand yourself. Wisdom is gained from truth. Discord within creates disharmony that breaks trust. When you feel incomplete and search for the answers outside, it is at this point that you are being called to turn inwards. When you forget the true self it can feel like you have nothing to offer life. To recover trust within is to be honest without hiding, rejecting or judging. This is the drive which will untether you and allow you to live a higher potential. Surrendering to all that you are is acceptance and this aligns you to the way of your fire. Belief gained from truth comes from authority within. When you have little belief within then you will seek this from an external authority. Being able to deliver all that is in you builds trust in yourself again. Trust is to live what is real to you and to surrender to every calling that you have for this will bring you to purpose. Where there is resistance to this there is pain. Living light is to turn attention inwards and to follow this truth.

GUIDANCE   You may find yourself struggling to understand what it means to turn inwards as you are so used to focusing on the external world around you. To do this you firstly relax and be; this is not with force but similar to the way you would be when you are taking time out. Let the mind wander and when you give this enough time the inner chattering will slow down. When you let go of trying to go inwards you may start to become aware of how you feel, how you are experiencing the physical body and what are the thoughts that fill the mind. Take time to 'see' yourself. All that you see is what is real for you and in the seeing you are listening to what you carry. Used consistently this starts to train your focus that clears a path to turning attention inwards again.

4.

To create life in a new way is to open to the true self.

Courage is needed to live fully as you have learnt to hide truth. You lose hope when you fear yourself. You realise hope when you regain trust within. Through the shadows the higher call becomes dull and so self-belief is replaced by looking towards external goals in the search for completion. In oneness of being there is completion where there is no longer a separation from the natural state. To find out what is real is the task. Through facing pain you alleviate that which is a cruel fight. To create life in a new way is to open to the true self. To live reality unlimited is to know the higher aspect of you.

GUIDANCE   What is real begins in the heart. To know what is meaningful to you comes with what touches you. Take a moment to consider what has touched you today, what made a lasting impression. You may not find this easy to do. To feel moved by our experiences is given little time and value. You cannot compare yourself to these experiences with anyone else because that which is true for you, may not be for another. Remember through this day what has brought emotion to the heart, what has moved you? This is what you are being urged to remember, through allowing yourself to feel; you come to the sense of what is true for you.

5.

*You forget how to accept what you have become and to believe
what you are being shown from within.*

In life you learn to grow your innate powers, to be all that you can be and to live a higher potential. The heart´s wish is to return to the essence of you and realise the Holy within. To truly find hope and live your aspirations is to come into the higher self. To break through the illusions that create the hardness in life is to open the self to inner light. In living, you can bring the brightness of you. To free is to emerge from behind the mask. To surrender to the inner process is to feel all that you are. You forget how to accept what you have become and to believe what you are being shown from within. To forget causes the wandering in life. To follow inner light awakens the drive of will to evolve truth in the highest way. Learning about all that you are is the prayer.

GUIDANCE   A collective pressure exists in life that leads you to compare yourself to everything around you. This phenomenon is crippling to higher development, so much so you do not believe in yourself. That which is being urged for you to remember is that your life can be like no other. When you yearn to be like another you turn away from the essence of you and search to be something you are not. You already have everything inside of you but it waits for you to accept it as the core of you. To reach the highest dream begins with what is in you right now and this cannot be acquired from outside of you.

6.

You are brought to life to gain more experiences, to strengthen you in order to grow light.

To regain trust is a careful process. In the hardness of life it is a challenge to see that the tenderness of light cannot be rushed, for this is where true joy and peace are. To trust this higher sensitivity is to witness the true power of life. Empowerment does not come with force or aggression. To live truth feels a risk, you must first have courage to open to treason created within. You are brought to life to gain more experiences, to strengthen you in order to grow light. Without trust you are unconfident in your abilities. Living from truth brings belief back to you. Through bad experiences you fall to the hardness that is created in you and this is a battle. You are weakened when the sadness of life sways the mind to follow what is outside of you. Through seeing this shadow you come to the true self.

GUIDANCE   Through the work of connecting people with their higher self a constant reminder is shown that life does not have to be this hard. Your innate wisdom knows that suffering is an illusion for your potential is great. You may question why you have to have such difficult experiences? Why you have to feel the ache within? You may want to run away from what comes towards you. The healing process shows that what comes your way you are ready for. In doubt and worry you feel overwhelmed but know that you are given this experience not to break you but to help you grow to the higher potential.

7.

The rupture inside of you is healed through belief in the heart.

Such a fall from the true self creates a profound effect on the essence of who you are. To trust is to open to all of creation and to not fight it. Out of fearing pain you began to lose trust. When you forget the higher path that is within, you became lost to misery. All inner treason comes from a personal pain. To hide is to fear showing all that you are and to live separately from the true self. Living without the higher aspect of you casts you from truth and so fear is what you promote. The rupture inside of you is healed through belief in the heart. To feel the ache of the past teaches you how you became weaker. Out of this realisation you know the humanness of being. The joy of living comes about from truth, for it is truth that leads you to the path of purpose. To find what is real inside of you means you cannot escape pain. This begins with knowing how you became what you are today.

GUIDANCE No-one deserves to be in pain. Life is not conspiring to make you suffer. When the heart became restricted from functioning in its full capacity it affected the way we cope with pain. The heart is strong and when empowered can overcome anything. When you feel hurt, it is not the pain that is hard to bear but the fact that you struggle to open the heart in it. In a true state the heart is able to accept everything because without restriction it is the connection to the life-giving force which has the ability to absorb any process no matter how painful or intense it may be.

8.

When you became powerless by not knowing yourself you became lost.

Distraction from light has been fundamental to the lack of care that has evolved in life. You forget light where there is corruption in the pursuit for external gratification. To live truth is to be in the sovereignty of being where there lays no question over who has authority. When you became powerless by not knowing yourself you became lost. Here is the loss of ability to be aware of what you are bringing to life. To realise light you are being asked to be conscious and take responsibility of all that you are. When you follow the truth of another you cannot know from within. You cannot be exactly the same as another. Life is not asking you to only see the hardship in life, but to realise that which is beyond it. The higher wish of the true self is to know what you yearn for, and that is wholeness. To realise empowerment comes from within and this brings a new path.

GUIDANCE   Within you is a vastness that is waiting to be explored. This concept that we already come with everything we need, all the understanding we could ask for still remains a mystery to many. This knowing manifests when you surrender to the world within you. For so long you prioritise the world outside of you to be of great value but this cannot reach the radiating light that you hold. You come with wisdom and all truth is in you. You have knowing when you break out of what you think you are and become the explorer of you.

9.

You must face pain not for punishment or to prolong suffering but to free from the illusion of fear.

Living to preserve yourself creates shaky foundations in the soul. To live free is to be free from fear and pain. Important messages are given to you through understanding pain. In the true self there is no guilt, shame or regret for this is who you are in that moment and you follow it for all it is. To have trust is to know that in the light and dark aspects of you there is a unique expression a higher intelligence. You attain trust by staying interested in what is inside of you and how you became to be this. Look to both what is pleasurable and what is pain, to accept all expressions as essential to what you are now. To learn about inner struggle is to have forgiveness within the heart. Forgiveness cannot exist when you cannot accept all heart impulses. Achieving light comes out of surrendering to what is true for you and to not fight it. Through facing darkness you find light. You must face pain not for punishment or to prolong suffering but to free from the illusion of fear. From this you begin to learn how to master yourself.

GUIDANCE   When you experience discomfort it is at this point that you are called to see yourself. The discomfort you feel is not a warning for you to shut down, its purpose is in fact the opposite, for it is preparing you. How? In the physiology of your being you start to become heightened, this may come in the form of anxiety, physical pain or tension, there are many ways that the body begins to show you that it needs attention. At this time, listen to yourself. Give this discomfort attention and when you do you begin to change the very way in which you heal. The body is so used to you ignoring it that the sentiment to not abandon yourself at this time sends a powerful message through you. You begin to change reality from being one of helplessness to belief in the higher intelligence of your being.

10.

When trust is lost, the ability to create reality becomes lost also.

When you come from a place of powerlessness then you cannot create a powerful life but you will seek to preserve yourself. To awaken power is to know the higher aspects within and to walk this path. When trust is lost, the ability to create reality becomes lost also. The battle for the true self must be conscious and willing to see truth. This path is very different to that which has been the outer reality. Forgetting truth makes you betray yourself and to fight that which is the Holy aspect within you.

GUIDANCE   How you are living life is not wrong or right. Being lost reflects the connection you have to higher hope inside of you. The origin of you has the ability to be known by you and to guide you to the highest purpose. Realising what you feel regarding how you trust is important. What you believe in has more value to you than what I or anyone else can show you. The question to ask is do you trust yourself? To regain trust within is to no longer be a stranger to yourself but to be in sacred union that is powerful.

11.

Self-belief is a hard path to follow if you look outside for it.

Self-belief is a hard path to follow if you look outside for it. To create meaning in life from external sources cannot open the heart fully but merely create respite. Trust leaves you when you become lost in a fight outside. To follow that which is outside of you is a daunting task and can never end for this is no true fight to win. In the seeds of pain you turn away from inner knowing and all self-trust is oppressed. With pain remaining in the heart you struggle for freedom and live out karma. In opening from the heart can there be trust within. That which is a clear path to the heart became lost in the distress of pain. The ability to forgive yourself and others comes from heart sensitivity. In despair forgiveness becomes hidden and there lies little hope. Inner healing can light the way. To master within you have to take the reins of life.

GUIDANCE   What is real for you lies in what you think, feel and believe. In life you are used to being given information of how you should be in the world. We are shown endless doorways to something better than what we are. To strengthen belief comes out of inner knowing, not in comparison to what you are being shown outside of you but completely apart from it. When you follow what is outside of you sooner or later you will feel wanting as you base yourself on a foundation that is not built by you. You can hear the truth of another and this may resonate with you but do not forget to connect with your experience.

12.

What is real comes from opening to the inner fire.

There are endless distractions from facing truth within. To escape and distract in endless external pursuits can only take you so far. It becomes a wish to move away from what is real and live for that which is outside of you. You do not acquire your fire out of the accumulation of power externally. This leads to a path of selfishness and creates treason within. Suffering is the inevitable outcome. Trying to escape what's in you creates grief for you mourn the light that is lost. To be all that you are and to find self-belief you need to free the internal struggle. What is real comes from opening to the inner fire. To come to this, you must break the pattern of ignoring that which is painful. It is in your hands that you create the life you lead. When you live with fear you remain lost and stay within a time bound restricted existence. To be the light is the freedom that lives into the brightness of you and this delivers empowerment.

GUIDANCE   In life we are learning to breathe. The inner fire is fuelled by the magnificence of light. To know this state is to create from what is real in you. The fire is the alignment of an open heart, strength of will and the higher potential. This is not beyond you or anyone if you wish it. This begins from inner knowing and to break down all the borders within that limit you from reaching your fire. This is the prayer.

13.

That which you came to do in the higher self is to unburden your being of all that makes you heavy.

The fabric of culture is based on the fact that you do not trust what lies within you. This is what inevitably encourages you to follow another to feel safe. Without inner light great apprehension and hopelessness is born. That which you came to do in the higher self is to unburden your being of all that makes you heavy. But you become weary in the battle and a slave to fear. To return power within is to open to the Holy for this higher aspect of you derives from the hallowed truth. In higher living what is true knows no fight or discord in itself. Turning inwards is the path to recover trust in the self. Paying attention to managing inner sentiments brings the Holy.

GUIDANCE   Through the commitments of life it is easy to feel that giving yourself attention is over indulgent, unnecessary and purposeless. What becomes the priority is doing and manifesting tangible outcomes. To approach life this way cannot solve the lack of care in the world and yet we give all our attention to it. This teaching shows you that to change reality for the highest good is to unburden the weight that you carry in the heart. Finding ways to release pain that is carried opens the heart. Every time you do this life becomes lighter for you and us all.

Summary of Teachings

1. Life is created from your own hands and this comes from truth.

2. In true being you are incorruptible for here the Holy derives.

3. Living light is to turn attention inwards and to follow this truth.

4. To create life in a new way is to open to the true self.

5. You forget how to accept what you have become and to believe what you are being shown from within.

6. You are brought to life to gain more experiences, to strengthen you in order to grow light.

7. The rupture inside of you is healed through belief in the heart.

8. When you became powerless by not knowing yourself you became lost.

9. You must face pain not for punishment or to prolong suffering but to free from the illusion of fear.

10. When trust is lost, the ability to create reality becomes lost also.

11. Self-belief is a hard path to follow if you look outside for it.

12. What is real comes from opening to the inner fire.

13. That which you came to do in the higher self is to unburden your being of all that makes you heavy.

FACE YOUR PAIN AND
EXPERIENCE RELEASE

UNDERSTAND
that your natural state is not suffering

LEARN
how pain is the doorway to the potential
of the true self

BELIEVE
that beyond pain is truth

1.

Suffering is not caused by the existence of pain but by
the fear of facing it.

In everyday life there is little questioning to whether what lies within you can combat fear. In accepting you are fated to be overwhelmed by fear you pass this sentiment on from generation to generation. The foundation of culture becomes built on the fact that fear and suffering must always be a part of life and that we personally can do little to eradicate it. The higher potential is far from this reality for you exist in a fearless state. To understand pain you must look at the reasons why it is there. It occurs to highlight an imbalance within. Choosing to escape, suppress or run away has been the coping strategy for many. By understanding the nature of pain you can be helped to move past the need to escape it. The energy of pain, if ignored can be like a parasite; it feeds off intolerance and fear of it. It is this resistance to pain that creates suffering. Suffering is not caused by the existence of pain but by the fear of facing it.

GUIDANCE   Acknowledging that you do not wish to ignore what's in you anymore is a catalyst to bringing about a new way. Pain is a part of you, it is the inner voice wanting to speak to you but you have not been listening. This is about giving yourself attention the way that you may give to another who needs comfort. Feel the sentiments of support and love that you would give to a distressed child. Maybe you have to repeat this many times before you find this quality within you. If you ignore the inner reality over a long period of time you will need patience in order to regain the trust of this higher sensitivity. If you do not give up in this challenge you can change the way you experience life.

2.

The intensity of pain acts as a benchmark to whether there is a deeper life lesson for personal growth.

Pain is a guidepost when there is a need to resolve something within that waits to be healed. It is the doorway to a wound that is held deep within you. When pain was originally created you were not able to consciously integrate it and so it could not come to resolve. If you find that pain returns its purpose is to give you the opportunity for this experience to heal. The intensity of pain acts as a benchmark to whether there is a deeper life lesson for personal growth. Trying to escape intense pain will not make it go away for it will continue to return one way or another to teach you the life lessons for you to grow, this is karma. Karma is creations innate way that ties you to an unresolved wound and it remains because it is essential for you to come to balance and growth. The resistance to pain occurs because you feel you are not able to deal with it therefore you are tied to this karmic cycle and this can be carried over life times if it is not healed.

GUIDANCE   When it feels you are doing everything right to make pain go away and it continues this can mean it has been with you a long time. You may ask why this occurs? Life is bringing to you in the best possible way the higher teachings that your being needs to evolve towards light. Without this intensity you would continue to ignore this potential in you. When pain rises then this is life's way of saying that you are ready to see it and resolve it. Healing the deeper imbalances to why this pain exists helps release its hold on you. Healing retrieves a lost power that is masked by your pain.

3.

The purpose of karma is to remedy the original wound, to release it or transform its energy to re-align the self to its higher sensitivity again.

Karma exists not as a punishment but to show you what is out of balance within. If not resolved over a long period of time the karmic tie can have very physical consequences. Depending on the intensity of the original wound, the stress or trauma causes direct impact on the energy body. Energy becomes dispersed by the intensity of the original pain and this imbalances the energy system. Blocked energies manifest as pain. The purpose of karma is to remedy the original wound, to release it or transform its energy to re-align the self to its higher sensitivity again. Higher sensitivity that lies beyond pain reveals truth. Through facing pain and understanding the original wound is truth released and the higher learning that the soul needs integrated. Without resolve karma remains and so you continue blind to the true self. To have courage to face pain brings clarity of your unique nature.

GUIDANCE When someone comes for healing it is concerning a block of some kind. This block can manifest as a physical pain, a powerful emotion, or a destructive behaviour.

Whatever it is it stops them from feeling comfortable within their being. The power of this block becomes concentrated and you can fixate on it so much that it can take the whole of your attention. This state is necessary to deal with its effects on you. It takes a lot of energy for you to deal with the effect of pain and to remain sensitive without resistance. In other words what you are requiring courage for is to witness the sensitive state of being whilst being challenged. Pain comes because you have moved away from the true way of being and dulled sensitivity. Through healing you are relearning to manage yourself again.

4.

*When you are unable to withstand internal conflict
indifference within is born.*

With many years of living with discord the loss of integrity feels a natural state. The loss of internal respect becomes vastly self-defeating and creates extreme internal conditions. When you are unable to withstand internal conflict indifference within is born. Because the soul nature is fragile, to cope with corruption you numb yourself to the experiences you are having, and suppress feeling. The collective experience of corruption and indifference makes you feel trapped in the illusion that life is overwhelming.

GUIDANCE   It is a natural reaction to feel uneasy in discomfort. What these teachings ask of you is to become aware of the way you inwardly respond. Indifference to seeing is a coping strategy as without it you have felt worse off. Indifference has helped you to not have to experience the parts of you that make you feel low. But these low parts are still there regardless and are affecting your well-being. When you go carefully and with support to open anything is possible. You don't want to see because it has not felt safe. To stay safe whilst opening is to go slowly and to not rush. You can find the right way for you. It is not how you do it that matters but that you do it.

5.

With self-responsibility relinquished combined with indifference you are led to powerlessness.

The symptoms of indifference are feelings of emptiness and so to fill this void you seek endless activities to escape it. Indifference disconnects a sense of responsibility. With self-responsibility relinquished combined with indifference you are led to powerlessness. If the foundation of you is in a self-corrupt place then you become powerless to hold ground and you are forced to look to another to feel safe. To look towards another for belief loses the true sense of meaning in life. By placing responsibility for yourself in another you become lost, needing external gratification and validation to feel secure. With personal power given away through indifference and corruption you become overshadowed.

GUIDANCE   Giving power away by not taking responsibility is self-defeating. When you look to another to carry you this is done because you believe it helps you to feel safer and worry less. This is not the case in fact to search endlessly for validation outside brings chaos into you. The search outside will be constant and so creates more worry for you. Fearing taking responsibility only adds to the struggle. To take responsibility is to believe in you for without belief you feel powerless. To have inner knowing is to break the cycle of indifference and when you follow truth, belief will come.

6.

To face pain invokes courage and so strengthens the will of being to face that which takes you to the brink of what you know.

It is because of a higher wisdom that you take the path of disempowerment. The experience of living in extreme internal conditions comes to facilitate awakening. The shadow parts are doorways to return to light. To face pain invokes courage and so strengthens the will of being to face that which takes you to the brink of what you know. Here lies the path to regaining self-belief. The purpose of suffering is not a permanent state of being but has come to move you towards light. You are not lost. To consciously move through hardship realises the higher states of being. You have the choice to see what is really in you, what you really fear and move past this illusion. What feels like suffering is giving you the opportunity for release, healing, and to return to wholeness.

GUIDANCE   We have become distracted in creating our lives for comfort, ease and pain free environments. When you are not pain free internally this cannot be achieved fully externally. When you create out of a false state life becomes filled with sterile, unreal experiences. In overcoming internal struggle you empower. To remain safe means you cannot move past the borders within and reach a higher potential. The next time you respond to something that you dislike or have an aversion to, remember that this is life giving you the opportunity to face a fear in you. When you take the harder path there is the potential to grow your light.

7.

The healing process helps you to have inner knowing and focuses energy to higher intentions.

In growing accustomed to powerlessness there is now the need for the facilitation of the healing process. Turning inwards feels a daunting task but you can look towards healers to guide the way. Many who have a deeper awareness of internal energies can help to unlock these inner truths and help heal wounds at the deepest level. Transforming energies is a lost skill and instruction from those who have walked this path is of great use to you. Through release in the healing process the energy freed up is needed to serve you. This strengthens the will force. The healing process helps you to have inner knowing and focuses energy to higher intentions. The power to create comes from the place of inner knowing, from the core of truth. Self-corruption and indifference shadows light from this truth. When self-integrity is weakened there is the loss of respect to yourself and your convictions. To regain integrity the journey starts within.

GUIDANCE   When seeking a healer or guide to help you often people wonder where to start. There is no methodology to it but to trust your instincts. Whether you are referred to someone or see a description of someone ask yourself do you wish to see this person? Close your eyes and take a moment to relax. When you imagine going to them do you feel an uplifting energy inside or do you feel that your energy is not going anywhere? If you don't feel anything or even get a sinking feeling then this is not the person for you. At the point you feel an uplifting energy, creating positivity and lightness within you then you know that this is a healthy response and may well be worth going for. This practice helps you grow your intuition of knowing the right path to take for you. Many people find that they experience their truth often within seconds of doing this practice. What seems to be a harder challenge is to trust this inner response and follow it. Know it is easy for doubt to follow but trust what you see is your truth.

8.

When you avoid pain in life, you lose the opportunity to empower yourself in the experience of an inner dying process.

The task to facing pain can feel overwhelming. Internal imbalance becomes the norm adapted to over years if not lifetimes. Facing the source of pain does not feel safe on both an emotional and energetic level. Because of not wanting to lose the emotional investment of who you believe you are, comes a fear of losing what is known. The transformative process of facing fear asks for you to have courage, for shedding of what is known is closely connected with a dying process. Walking towards the edge of what has been before and taking that leap of faith to the unknown has not been encouraged, understood or liked. When you avoid pain in life, you lose the opportunity to empower yourself in the experience of an inner dying process. Through the transformation of pain in healing you move past the borders of what you believe to be and open to that which is vital and new.

GUIDANCE   I imagine that to most people avoiding a dying process is greatly welcomed and yet here the teachings hold this rite of passage in high esteem to reaching our higher potential. What you are reminded of is that all fear within must be overcome to enter light of being, for in a true state you are fearless. What we don't understand we often want to move away from. Life cannot be truly lived until the fear of death and the dying process is intrinsically understood. The process of surrendering and letting go through the healing process is reflective of your response to the unknown. The fear of death does not exist when you live the wisdom of the light self.

9.

To be in optimum health the energy force within must
flow freely.

To achieve well-being, to grow into the potential of you means that facing pain cannot be bypassed for there can be no escape hatches. The act of ignoring pain within makes it grow stronger. All energies created want to expand and grow whether positive or negative in nature; if pain is left unchecked then it can disturb and eventually block the natural energy flow in the body. To be in optimum health the energy force within must flow freely. This principle lies behind many of the energy therapies that exist today, to achieve balance energy must move freely. Energy blocks have a direct effect on the harmony of your physical, emotional and mental state.

GUIDANCE   Health is like the natural inhalation and exhalation of breath, this knowing is effortless. You can experiment with this following practice. Notice the breath and feel into the rise and fall of the breath in this moment. What you are looking for is whether this movement feels freely flowing. For many this is not the case, you can feel restricted, tense or tight, you can have short, shallow or erratic breathing patterns. Why? This is reflective of our journey to wholeness and wellbeing. Peace is when we are free and when the flow of our breath is at ease. If every day you remember to take a few minutes to remind yourself to take deeper, fuller and slower breaths you send a message to the higher self that you have not forgotten the value you place to reaching harmony within you.

10.

The nature of the will force is to serve and if it cannot serve you then it will look outside of its self and adapt itself to serve others.

Through the loss of inner knowing you weaken will power. The will force needs to serve something for its purpose is to put into motion what is asked to be created. It is the driving force behind what you express into the world and forms and shapes the reality that you wish for. The clearer you are in your intentions the easier it is for the will to serve you effectively. In the fear of going within and the loss of knowing, the strength of intention becomes weak and unclear. Sense of purpose becomes lost as you stray ever further from inner truth. The nature of the will force is to serve and if it cannot serve you then it will look outside of its self and adapt itself to serve others. Without a strong sense of self the ability to create an outer reality that you believe in wanes. When you lose belief then you experience the outer reality with indifference.

GUIDANCE   The ability that you have to influence the world around you is powerful. Each one of us has this potential but very few live empowered lives. Knowing why we adapt to a false self can be helpful. You come with a will force that belongs to you and is designed to be of service to you. To have a strong will does not come with aggression and has nothing to do with bullying life for your needs. I speak of a state that comes from a higher principle for when you work out of a place of self-belief based on truth it brings a deep knowing that you have all that you need to create the world you want to live in. You adapt because you have lost the connection to yourself and so seek others to build the knowing of you. This traps you and keeps you wanting. To live with a free will is to be in sovereignty. This comes when you allow the true self to lead.

11.

*Self-preservation and polarity ceases when there is no
separation from within and you live out of the oneness
of being.*

In a true state there is the experience of no polarities, no
higher or lower states, no forcing or giving, no pleasure or
displeasure. This wisdom is the essence of care. Careful practice is a state of being rather than an experience to switch
on or off. To live with polarity creates struggle. In compart-
mentalising within and existing through the duality of right
and wrong, good and bad life becomes a struggle. External
rules and values are created for praise or condemnation. Life
becomes contained and restricted just like the inner reality.
True care cannot exist from here, for it has no borders but
lives with the awe of life and its preciousness. It is the sweetness of life. Self-preservation and polarity ceases when there
is no separation from within and you live out of the oneness
of being. Through this sweetness in life love can exist and
flourish.

GUIDANCE   To live polarised which is the opposite state
of oneness you create an image of yourself that is fed from
discord. Here is an example of this, you feel frustrated that
you have not got money and so you yearn for money. You learn
to long for the opposite of what you don't have. Living this way
is a habit and a psychological construct that has formed a way
of being. If I am not what I desire then I will lose myself in the
search for what I think is desirable. You distract from feeling
pain by chasing the image of what health is. Living in polarity

prevents you from accepting who you are and surrendering to change. When you stop longing for what you don't have you can give attention to what you are running away from. To be real is to know what you are, and to know this, for it has something to show you.

12.

Sensitivity and tenderness is key to careful living.

That which derives from sensitivity creates the knowing of how to live a true life. All that is not this creates an imbalance of some kind. Tenderness cannot be bought or borrowed; it comes from inner knowing and the belief in the power of the vulnerability of the true nature. Then love can be. Sensitivity and tenderness is key to careful living. Through personal resolve can balance and harmony be restored. The collective experience of corruption has given a belief that struggle and suffering is a common place experience. Suffering is a transitory process, one that is created to return to the true nature. The potential to create paradise on earth is unfolding in life all the time. To return to this state of completion is to come to eternal joy that is a higher longing. You came not to suffer but to create the paradise within you.

GUIDANCE   It is common knowledge that many people have difficulty sharing their feelings. What you may not understand is that this acts as a mirror to what is happening inside of you. This means that you have difficulty in sharing to yourself that which is real in you. For example think of an issue that has been a point of concern for you, something you try to push to the back of the mind. Now the aim of this is to be as honest as you can, don't hold back, ask yourself what is really going on for you. What are you struggling with? It may help to say it out loud. You can start sentences with 'This makes me feel....' Or 'I don't want to feel...' Sooner or later you will see that you are realising what you really feel about this issue. This helps you to share a true process with yourself. Not because you can't do this but because you have got used to sharing what you want to hear and not listening to all that is true within.

13.

With this super sensitivity you are open to the many spheres of life that are beyond the physical.

When life is lived with the heart fully open and in balance there is a shift out of the physical world and so connection is made in a very different way. By sensing through the heart you are not bound by the physical, instead you are free to make connection with the resonance of life rather than what which you see with the naked eye. With this super sensitivity you are open to the many spheres of life that are beyond the physical. When open, the heart is able to explore its surroundings for the purpose of connection, exploration and experience. It is able to intuit and to be touched by the world around it. The heart has the ability to 'tune' itself into the other. This tuning is based on a vibrational level, it allows for movement of frequencies in and out of it which emanate in all life. It has the ability to interpret that which is not bound by its physical aspect. It connects to the resonance of matter and in this resonance a wider range of information can be detected.

GUIDANCE   Interconnectedness means the free movement between all aspects of you. You have a physical, emotional, mental and energetic body. In the true self there is a natural harmony between all these states. To one level or other you have become separated, divided and live with restrictions within the layers of yourself. This is what it means to be fragmented. Each part of you wants to express itself freely. Opening is to dissolve these borders within you by lifting the resistance to expression. To come to wholeness is in accepting that you are a sensitive being that is here to explore the greatness of you in all colours.

Summary of Teachings

1. Suffering is not caused by the existence of pain but by the fear of facing it.

2. The intensity of pain acts as a benchmark to whether there is a deeper life lesson for personal growth.

3. The purpose of karma is to remedy the original wound, to release it or transform its energy to re-align the self to its higher sensitivity again.

4. When you are unable to withstand internal conflict indifference within is born.

5. With self-responsibility relinquished combined with indifference you are led to powerlessness.

6. To face pain invokes courage and so strengthens the will of being to face that which takes you to the brink of what you know.

7. The healing process helps you to have inner knowing and focuses energy to higher intentions.

8. When you avoid pain in life, you lose the opportunity to empower yourself in the experience of an inner dying process.

9. To be in optimum health the energy force within must flow freely.

10. The nature of the will force is to serve and if it cannot serve you then it will look outside of its self and adapt itself to serve others.

11. Self-preservation and polarity ceases when there is no separation from within and you live out of the oneness of being.

12. Sensitivity and tenderness is key to careful living.

13. With this super sensitivity you are open to the many spheres of life of beyond the physical.

WALK WITH FEAR AND DO NOT REJECT IT

UNDERSTAND
that running away from fear limits your potential

LEARN
that fear is a stepping stone to retrieving power

BELIEVE
beyond the borders within, you reach your
purpose

1.

Without fear you become complacent and lose momentum to why you are here.

Fear is a mighty teacher and yet in life you run away from it. Suppression and terror caused by fear have been tragic for human potential. Fear exists to help align you further to a higher power and not to disempower you. In its rightful place it paves the way to what you truly wish for. To walk with fear is to befriend it, hold it in high esteem as a truth that is asking you to realise light. Without fear you become complacent and lose momentum to why you are here. Fear is reacted to by fleeing or fighting and either direction brings turmoil. The reason for fear as a phenomenon is due to the treason that is created by yourself. Fear comes when self-belief is corrupted from countless times of betraying inner truth and not accepting the nature of you. You must realise that what lies beyond fear is the wisdom of the Holy expression calling for realisation. Fear begins the process and initiates the route back to the Holy presence within you.

GUIDANCE   What this teaching speaks of is every time you feel discomfort stop and be aware of yourself. To ignore discomfort within is being reinforced all around you, to get on, to stop making a fuss, to not be weak. Learning to encourage each other in a new way of being takes patience and this starts within you. Life giving impulses emanates from truth. Where there is discord is the showing that you are out of alignment. The next time you become aware of discomfort within you stop and be aware that what is happening is bringing you back to your truth.

2.

Without resolving the karmic tie, this truth and the energy which lies behind it cannot serve you.

The discomfort created by pain lifts you out of a 'normal' state of being and focuses the senses. You do not need to fear this process but accept that it is a very natural part of the body's preparation process. This is crucial to healing because it helps you to be ready to meet the charged energies that may follow. Through this preparation you harness power to help you release trapped energy. To face that which lies beyond fear now offers you the opportunity to release a part of you which up until this moment has been held on to. When the original wound was created your unique being became lost within the wound. Without resolving the karmic tie, this truth and the energy which lies behind it cannot serve you. Without facing pain there remains a fragmentation and disempowerment until you can open to all that you are in a safe and accepting way.

GUIDANCE   This is a powerful healing truth. That which feels like a burden is a treasure waiting for you to find. Having lost a part of you is what you retrieve when you understand the story behind the pain. What it seeks is release, to not remain hidden any longer and celebrate you. Each time you have the courage to stand alone and to feel and accept is a great achievement. Each moment you release pain you release the light of your story and this is truth. What is to be honoured is that you are your own hero. You win when you shine.

3.

The separation from the true state of being is no accident for you created it willingly and so grief follows.

The task is to feel into fear. Modern life creates many distractions and you follow others for a way out. To willingly give up responsibility by following another cannot eliminate the fear within you. The separation from the true state of being is no accident for you created it willingly and so grief follows. When there is commitment to not abandon yourself in fear then life can be lived with power. You have to ask whether in managing life, how much of it is being lived to strengthen the true self? The higher aspect of you lies within sensitivity but this is predominately resisted by the collective. Many other tasks are managed and life has been over-shadowed by earning and acquiring for external gain but none of this can solve or answer how to live without pain. In fear you form restrictions and limitations in the search for an external power. You become lost to the reasons of your downfall and start to blame others for why life is corrupt. Living life like this creates a movement away from a natural state in its higher potential.

GUIDANCE   An illusion in life tells you that you are a victim and that you are helpless in it. You believe this because of the level of despair and sadness that you have within but not because it is a truth. This reality check is not easy to swallow. In the true nature you know where power lies and this is in you. The process of grief remains within until you are whole again. Anger comes when you struggle to come to terms with your fragile soul, when you want to deliver much more than you are and you feel you have been cheated in some way. In this struggle we are learning to forgive ourselves and accept what we have become and take responsibility of creating a future we wish for.

4.

There is a strong potential that the energy that pain is linked to carries a heavy or toxic force and so a physiological, emotional and mental preparation is required.

To understand that pain is a necessary process you must learn what its true function is. Energetically pain acts as a threshold in preparing you to go deeper. It does this by bringing about a heightened awareness and this may make you feel uncomfortable. The discomfort is absolutely necessary for it is trying to get your attention. Pain is the trigger to show you that you need to now give time and attention to help you open to something deeper. Pain is preparing you, you are preparing yourself. It does this because this is the necessary state needed to face the deeper energies that are trapped within. There is a strong potential that the energy that pain is linked to carries a heavy or toxic force and so a physiological, emotional and mental preparation is required. This is pains objective. Depending on how long the wound has been carried or suppressed can determine the strength of this trapped energy. The charge of energy that lies beyond pain is looking for release and this is one of the essential processes in healing the self.

GUIDANCE   What this teaching shows is that the healing process is multi layered and such processes cannot be rushed. It is uncommon for people to know that they have many aspects of their being that need to be expressed to come to balance. Often people will force themselves out of the healing process because it is not quick enough. This is a whole new world, with every turn can be a new process revealed to you that needs time for you to adjust. For these processes to be integrated you must go slowly and not rush.

5.

Planning in this way is anti-being in life, restricting and limiting the exploration of you.

You are asked to feel into truth and to do this there can be no planned expectation. Planning in this way is anti-being in life, restricting and limiting the exploration of you. The creative fire cannot be contained for it stands a risk of being smothered. Over time you have become frightened of the true self where there is sadness in the heart from the knowing that you have betrayed the higher self. The stress experienced from pain effects the expression of the creative life force that emanates from the heart. To live free from restrictions within life fulfils its higher purpose. Within the hallowed place is the praising of supreme consciousness where you are wary of nothing.

GUIDANCE   Every time you attach to an outcome or have expectations you stifle life. Letting go of needing to know is a great spiritual challenge. This is to live in light. Let us make the differentiation; having inner knowing is not the same as the want of knowing what you will become. Inner knowing is the recognition of what is true for you in this moment's experience and the other is premeditated and tries to fix form. One flows and the other restricts. When you feel discomfort then you instantly want to fix and know how to control it. This higher lesson shows us that we are being asked to let go of fixing and replace it with inner knowing where you become aware of your response to life and accept what you are being shown.

6.

If there lays no belief internally then life becomes full of fear.

In rejecting fear a battle exists. It is through the call to observe yourself and to remember how to navigate through the place of fear that you surrender this fight. Such a powerful challenge triggers a way out of the flames and to recall how to ask out of you and not from another. When you fall, it feels as if following another is necessary to be carried. When you follow another then fear continues to exist and so this becomes reality. Through the true self united and free can life be truly managed. In the journey to wholeness is the battle in life to drive out hate. From fear, when it is left unchecked hate grows. If there lays no belief internally then life becomes full of fear. There can be no complacency when fear is present. There must be a knowing that, without watching it, you cannot grow and be who you are supposed to become. To witness the hallowed presence within is to challenge the space of time that traps you. To walk with fear is to find out how it has come to be. In the joining to internal power you free the essence of you from fear.

GUIDANCE The essence of belief resonates at a strong and light frequency which helps to reinforce trust. When there is little or no belief then you feel forced to follow another. You think that this is helping you but what happens is that you weaken the vibration of you for you have not solved the underlying reason of why self-belief went in the first place. You believe another when confidence is low. Confidence cannot be strengthened again until you are able to take responsibility of yourself. Through the healing process you have the possibility to learn why self-belief is low and grow it again. When the energy of self-belief is lacking then fear will grows in its place.

7.

You do not have to settle for what is shown to you but to manage reality.

Easily you forget light. In life there are all types of distractions and such a force has been detrimental to strengthening light. In the search for external power, you feel that you master, but this is only transitory. Many are guests to their truth, strangers to their light. The soul becomes fragile from the tiredness it endures. The external race is not a race you can ever win, for this place encourages wanting for the self alone and this causes a living hell away from a higher state of being. But in the fall is the potential for the brightness within to be illuminated. You do not have to settle for what is shown to you but to manage reality. To follow light lies the shining. Power is from truth, and love is created through the creative alliance of the true self. Through this you live love and create heaven on earth.

GUIDANCE   To deliver truth you must have absolute knowing of that which lies inside of you. To fine tune skills externally cannot give you light, this comes through feeling all the aspects of you. Seeing inside of you is a multi-faceted experience. Through the inner world you are being asked to see the movement of you, sensations, thoughts, feelings, the sound of you, the breath of you, your urges, your tensions all of these aspects are you. Go inside, notice if this is comfortable for you to do. Do not be disheartened if you only manage a short time. This is using awareness skills that have to be grown again just like growing a muscle you have not used before. Everything you see inside of you is what is real for you. Let the inner world inform you of who you are.

8.

The reason fear exists is to help move you out of what limits you.

Masking the truth creates fractures in the soul. This becomes unbearable to carry. Even when the opportunity to follow truth arises and the potential of coming close to whom you really are, you respond out of self-preservation. In rejecting fear, you reject yourself. The effect that this has in you can be desperation, for you abandon yourself in pain. In ignoring pain you lose the opportunity to master fear and become lost. The reason fear exists is to help move you out of what limits you. When you allow feeling what is within, hope appears. In this the decision to realise light above all and to lift into truth lays empowerment.

GUIDANCE   Higher teachings come to you when you are on the edge of what you know in yourself and you have to walk into the unknown. This challenge and all that it brings up in you brings the opportunity for you to realise that you are much more than you believe. Not knowing is what you fear the most. You are your greatest teacher. Continue to walk with fear for it is a higher intelligence and when you follow its expression it will take you by the hand and show you what lies beyond.

9.

That which comes out of a natural state is a new way of being which can never be the same as another.

To find purpose is to live out of a place of inner truth. When you face fear it is to bring the highest good. To join into the oneness of being you must move past fear by not rejecting it but allowing it to show you what it holds. To live away from the trap of time without karma holding you to the past, you can live truly from the true self. If you choose to reject fear then inner truth is lost, and you return to being caught in time and to the race of life. To live without the higher aspect free, you are unable to vitalise truth. The call is to remember, to follow yourself and become empowered from within.

That which comes out of a natural state is a new way of being which can never be the same as another. Acts of conformity are alien to the true self. In the higher self you do not fear and so there is no attachment for self-gain or loss. Without the chase for external power you could not have seen how to live and remember truth. The price of wanting power outside traps you and the way out is to awaken light and to not fear.

GUIDANCE   Discord within causes many distractions in life and you do not experience truly celebrating yourself. You become confused that anything to do with going within is a selfish act, that you will be too much for others to handle, or you will be too strong. To shine light does not come from the same place as this reality. To know yourself in light is the awakening to love. Empowerment is given a different interpretation in an aggressive culture. Celebrating you is opening to the gift of joy which has the ability to touch everyone around you. Imagine in your daydreams what you look like in your shining. Can you feel how this feels for you? When love celebrates you this has nothing to do with comparing or the achievements you have gained but from inner knowing that you are love and you are the celebration of life.

10.

The greatest fear is the death of the image of you; this becomes darkness and brings about heaviness in life.

Living is now a struggle and to transform life you must decide to live another way. To return to the fire of light is to let go of external attachments. The greatest fear is the death of the image of you; this becomes darkness and brings heaviness in life. In the negation of all that has been, can the glory of the true self follow its highest good and live out of its truth. In the persistent remembering of what is real for you can power be revived. In light you lose nothing for you do not seek to gain. The leap of faith is to trust into the light of being, for this is the true guide. To ignite the intrigue to the higher life, you light that which lies within you first. When you are free from the constructs of what you believe to be then you are free from burdens and can explore the true power that lies in the fire.

GUIDANCE   The loss of internal power breeds the sense that you are not in control. Truth is like a rock that creates strong foundations in you. So when the winds of change come from outside of you, you know how to stand strong in power. You can feel that you worry when you are not in light. Take a moment to observe the external pressures that create many uncertainties for you. What do you find yourself worrying about? Many people worry about what they believe they should be and how to maintain this at all cost. If you create not out of truth but to serve the beliefs of an external force you become trapped. The need to sustain another's belief is tiring and limiting. Let yourself not try to force these worries away but give them space. Ask if these worries are real for you and do you believe them? Differentiating between what means something to you and what confuses you will bring you back to the sense of you.

11.

In oneness can the cause be found to return to the shining
of the inner fire.

What is real and belongs to you is not given to you by another. In fear you follow and so truth cannot be realised through external sources. In the same way that you choose to follow you can choose not to. You cannot find completion and wholeness if you serve that which is outside of you. The higher call of life on earth is the wish to realise the true self. It is in its asking consciousness of light becomes real. In oneness their lives no separation, no dark, no light, no pain, no joy all just is. In the separation of the original state of oneness polarity came to exist. Light is realised again when no duality exists and you can see all is one. In oneness can the cause be found to return to the shining of the inner fire. All that you create has no price or value and there is no emphasis placed on what you are offering. All that remains to see is truth realised.

GUIDANCE   In becoming you are growing your will power. To stop and witness what is happening inside of you is essential to having a strong will, how you respond to life is valuable for you to see. For example notice what you sense is happening inside of you in response to what you have just heard. Are you open, resistant, confused, happy, inspired what are the sensations you feel? To know yourself you take the reins and slow everything down so that you understand what touches you and then you move from here. People fixate about what they feel they should think, say or do. You can feel unsure if another person has a reaction to something and you don't. This is your truth; everything you feel is unique to you. To accept all that is in you and live truth is to realise that you are a stranger to yourself and this is the greatest journey you can make, to get to know the mystery of you.

12.

Life forces must be directed; when you walk unconsciously then you are open to all manner of distractions.

Through life is the potential to rise to power within. To create out of your fire, where you are aligned with a free heart, mind and spirit is to know freedom. In living truth lay's the depths of peace. Through the heart is the need to move out of falling and to realise the creative light in its unlimited power. To immerse into every spectrum of the feeling range allows for the freeing of love within. What lies in you matters. Such a process in modern life is out of style, replaced with the vanities of external gratification and influences that dictate truth. What is fundamental to the strength of your being is the power you create in living. Life forces must be directed; when you walk unconsciously then you are open to all manner of distractions. When this power is reinforced by not forgetting yourself and following your truth, then there will lay an invincible power of will that can cast its light that banishes all sense of doubt. What was once mighty within, has had life times of being oppressed and corrupted and so firstly you breathe out your pain in order to lift you higher.

GUIDANCE Every moment you can be experiencing many things that seek attention. The internal stimulus can be sensations, sounds, impulses, smells, tensions, emotions and thoughts. What becomes a strong habit is you want to tend that which is outside of you; it is what you have been giving your attention to for a long time. To open to the impressions that you have of life and to bring consciousness to inner knowing is to go carefully. Allow yourself to experiment. Take five minutes at any point of each day and allow your attention to move from the external stimulus and then back to the sensations within. Externally could be sounds, activity or movement. Internally can be the movement of the breath, sensations or impulses. In this time notice the level of concentration needed to move in and out of you. This is you becoming conscious of moving between the inner and outer realities. To remember to go within takes practice.

13.

There is the belief that truth is only created from outside of you.

By following within, to listen and adhere to the truth of inner knowing is the showing of the true being. There is the belief that truth is only created from outside of you. The living force that resides within is the potential of empowerment and you are being asked to take responsibility. Without turning within devastation is created causing the phenomena of fear. Fear is not the menace or the enemy for it comes out of the higher meaning of grief. The fight has been against yourself, the fear of the true expression. Only through the realisation of inner truth can creation come out of the knowing from a higher place. To not cast this you are lost to seeking belief through the games of life. In forgetting the task of coming you have to figure out how to live again. Through the conscious asking of this pursuit can there be the negation of walking blindly in life.

GUIDANCE   Forgetting the vastness that lies inside of you, creates a reality that all that matters is your persona in the external world. What you crave outside cannot satisfy the wish in you for wholeness. That which has been tragic for the higher potential is the demand that the external life is of greatest value. Without internal harmony peace cannot be a reality externally. You are able to tap into subtle realities that exist out with the physical planes. To begin inside of you creates the world you wish to live outside of you.

Summary of Teachings

1. Without fear you become complacent and lose momentum to why you are here.

2. Without resolving the karmic tie, this truth and the energy which lies behind it cannot serve you.

3. The separation from the true state of being is no accident, for you created it willingly and so grief follows.

4. There is a strong potential that the energy that pain is linked to carries a heavy or toxic force and so a physiological, emotional and mental preparation is required.

5. Planning in this way is anti-being in life, restricting and limiting the exploration of you.

6. If there lays no belief internally then life becomes full of fear.

7. You do not have to settle for what is shown to you but to manage reality.

8. The reason fear exists is to help move you out of what limits you.

9. That which comes out of a natural state is a new way of being which can never be the same as another.

10. The greatest fear is the death of the image of you; this becomes darkness and brings about heaviness in life.

11. In oneness can the cause be found to return to the shining of the inner fire.

12. Life forces must be directed; when you walk unconsciously then you are open to all manner of distractions.

13. There is the belief that truth is only created from outside of you.

TAKE RESPONSIBILITY

UNDERSTAND
that you transform reality by not following
another and settling for what you are shown

LEARN
that gaining power externally cannot bring
empowerment but forces you to live another's
ideals

BELIEVE
to return to light comes from the sensitivity
of being

1.

*To come back to the true sense of being is a constant mission,
for you have developed habits that search for answers
outside of you.*

In the pressures of modern life there is little personal space. Pain and suffering is passed from generation to generation, forming an accumulation of fear in the heart. In order to heal, creating yourself is a conscious act for this journey. To break the cycle of discord that has become modern reality you must look within and not be led by another. You break the cycle of despair when you take responsibility of your part of its creation. Finding the way back to inner light can be alluding as doubt and resistance are companions. To come back to the true sense of being is a constant mission, for you have developed habits that search for answers outside of you. You need a safe space to learn about the terrain within. As with any unfamiliar territory, orientation of how to navigate yourself is needed.

GUIDANCE   In a time where everything is expected to happen quickly and where you are encouraged to not stand out from the crowd the subtle pressures of life creates a stream that goes against opening. To open you have to stand alone and slow life down. The most powerful experience that challenges you to return to light is to face loneliness. No one wants to leave the safety of the tribe, to walk out into the wilderness alone. You believe it is not safe, that you do not have it in you to stand apart. A person's spirit that is fighting to free itself from fear is beautiful. Courage is in you but it is not until you reach the edge of all you have ever known can you see it. To know courage is not necessarily to know it before you turn inwards but it is something that you realise you have along the way.

2.

In taking responsibility you seek to unblock what hides the heart from leading again.

It is through the essence of the heart force that brings the courage to accept all that you feel. This expression is not a pre-meditated, prepared or formulated act but is vital, new and resonates from hope. The first step to opening the heart is to discover what is real in you. Self-belief comes from feeling from the heart and this cannot be reached outside of you. Taking responsibility is seeing and not rejecting or avoiding what you see for this way transforms life. Fulfilment in life is transitory and not lasting without the heart fully active. In taking responsibility you seek to unblock what hides the heart from leading again. To navigate the inner realm, you must let go of all expectations of what you expect to see, for the place of thought limits you. The place of the heart resonates at a different frequency and does not come from thought. Your feelings are like catching something in the wind for it emanates with subtle vibrations.

GUIDANCE   Sensitivity lies within the essence of the heart. To come to the state of inner knowing you must be able to hear what is in the heart. Why is this so difficult? Resistance to uncomfortable feelings makes you reject and even fear seeing anything that does not feel good. We pick up that the collective feeling shows us that we don't know how to cope with discord. Imagine everyone you see is dealing with their own discord and also not able to share it comfortably. To open is essential to not just wellbeing but to the potential of becoming the true self. You cannot avoid feeling uncomfortable on this journey but it is through the release of what blocks you from the true essence of you that power comes.

3.

You try to hold on to things that can never really be owned.

Many are driven in life for the prospect of gaining and accumulating for themselves. You try to hold on to things that can never really be owned. Such constructs trap you in attachment to how you see yourself. To understand what is driving you forward is of great importance to transforming reality. To cope with the discord in the self and the world, you conform, rebel or fight but these ways cannot reach far for the old structures remain. That which is held on to creates a power struggle. To come back to the true sense of self, you must learn how to transcend this struggle. To co-create reality from the true expression of being you must realise that empowerment does not lie in achieving externally, for it comes from within when the noise of the soul quietens.

GUIDANCE   Where commodity is an accepted way of life, then to understand this higher truth is challenging. This spiritual seeing is fundamental to living the greater potential of you. Each time you believe you own anything you encourage the sentiments of attachment. To attach brings about feelings of holding on, to believe that which is outside of you is fundamental to which you are. This is mirrored in the healing process, each time you believe you have to be a certain way you attach to this and fear the loss of it. For example someone comes and asks to find out what blocks them from moving on from a relationship. The healing shows that they identify that to feel happy they need recognition from another. They hold on to the person in order to help them cope with the fear that without them they cannot find happiness. This is the essence of healing; you fear losing something that you attach to because it serves the wound in you and you can't let it go. When you learn to master loss in yourself you become free.

4.

Connection that comes from within is giving and does not act out of the need for itself.

Life has become divided into what is owned and what is not, what can be shared and what is held back. To seek answers to problems from a disconnected place is futile. Connection that comes from within is giving and does not act out of the need for itself. Life can never seem enough when there is a race to climb an external ladder. To want to be more than what you are, is the movement for self-gratification alone. Life becomes an uneasy place. Reality is a struggle created by the restrictions that you place on yourself. All constraints force you to fit into something and to follow within its limitations. If you are to change this flow, this struggle must be witnessed within you. In realising what is coming up for you, then trust can manifest. The task is to remove the blocks to the brilliance of you. From here reality is transformed to a balanced and natural order within.

GUIDANCE   When you experience insecurity, when you feel unsure of what you believe in or how to follow yourself become aware of this moment. What comes from a loving and free space inside of you is free of worry and discord. When you are confused then this is because you genuinely feel that something is not right and not because you are stuck. This can be the hardest thing for people to understand, you start to believe that you are confused out of a weakness within and ignore the authenticity of what you feel. The truth is you are confused because something has not fired you and you must decide to let it go or do something about it. What comes from a true place comes with clearness or it is not your truth. Truth does not come from force it just is. This is how you know when something resonates with your unique being you are touched by it in a light way.

5.

Through the arts, the heart is given permission to lead, having licence to dream.

Within the constructs of a restricted reality is the escape into a counter culture of creative expression. Through the arts, the heart is given permission to lead, having licence to dream. For many its expression gives great relief and comfort through the struggle of existence. To understand that to be in touch with the heart centre is being in touch with the hallowed presence of being. Believing that the supersensitive world is out of reach creates many images of what is Holy but the true expression comes from inner knowing.

GUIDANCE   It is common knowledge that you can be moved by the sentiments created by music and the arts. The essence of creativity of the heart moves in this arena. When you struggle to know what it feels like to move from the place of the heart then let yourself listen to a piece of music, read a poem or look at a piece of art that touches you. When you do this then close your eyes and feel the sensations that arise in you. What this teaching shows you is that everyone can feel into their heart space but you may need a little help in detecting this place in a stronger way. What moves and touches you is what is real to you. Living life without being touched by the world around you is to live only a part of the greater experience of your potential.

6.

It is not the shadow self that creates disempowerment but the pressure to achieve another's ideal.

In the drudgery of life you become despondent but it is what lies beyond darkness that brings illumination. Through the countless times of falling, pain and harm is created. That which is found when you face the shadows of the soul has been strongly misunderstood by the collective experience. It is not the shadow self that creates disempowerment but the pressure to achieve another's ideal. Order, harmony and the tranquillity of life cannot be given or found outside of you. Order cannot be imposed or forced on you from external sources for if it is, it will be disempowering by nature. Your experience of what is true must come from you to create a reality that is free from discord. That which now grows from hardship gives you the potential to find the hallowed presence that lies beyond it. This is how release comes. The creative life force is invoked from the intensity that is created from these extreme conditions. In this hardship lies the threshold of the hallowed presence.

GUIDANCE   When life is lived for external gain then you will not be free of comparing yourself to another. You will always fall short of completion when you look outside for it. When not in your true state at some point you come to discord. This insecurity forces you to compare any downfall to another. You live a powerless state because you remain attached to what others may think of you. To walk your path you must learn to stand alone. You can feel that each time you go within is the fear of being alone and so run back to the safety of others. Each time you do this you lose the opportunity to retrieve your power. You can find help to do this but what matters is that you do it.

7.

Experiencing life through the feeling body allows the world to read what you need and in turn bring that to you.

Learning about the fragility and sensitivity in you regains truth of how to live. It is through seeing suffering that willingness can be found to break this cycle of pain. In the separation of the heart force the sentiments to relate to yourself and the world became lost. Feelings are what connect you to the sensitivity of the world. When structures impose what life should be then insensitivity is evoked. Giving priority to feeling enables the return to higher work. Experiencing life through the feeling body allows the world to read what you need and in turn bring that to you. This is co-creation with life. In direct experience of what lies beyond pain can truth and light be realised. It is the inner realm that is superior to this realisation.

GUIDANCE   Life reads you through the way that you sense the world. What you show the world is what life believes you want. The subtle forces of life do not come with discord and fragmentation, it does not know this way of holding back. What it sees in you whether you are creating out of the true self or not is what it brings towards you. This is the law of attraction, when you are not in touch with the true essence of you then what you really want cannot come your way. This is why it is of great service to you to have the courage to show all that you are so that life can understand you clearly and bring you what you need to support the shining.

8.

Indifference appears when hope is lost but it is your unique soul journey that returns power and confidence to you.

The story of the soul becomes the beacon to light. Indifference appears when hope is lost but it is your unique soul journey that returns power and confidence to you. It is pointless to judge and compare this journey with another for all are created uniquely. To understand and be guided in reclaiming integrity you must take responsibility of what you are. There are many hurdles if you become lost to shame and guilt in the fall but this is to learn the teachings of the unfolding experience of life. Shame and guilt is an expression of a punishing reality that is not in alignment to higher truth. The reality of you is in your hands no matter how far there is to climb. To lift higher is to have the willingness to see what lies within you.

GUIDANCE   Life is enhanced by the longing in the heart of man. Why? With every sincere showing of the sentiments in the heart, joy is created out of our sight. To cry is the beauty of love. It is your soul journey you are learning to celebrate and to remember to not resist the truth of who you are. When you let yourself feel all the colours that you come with, the heart and life opens with relief and joy. To hold back feeling does not serve you or life. To feel is to become aware of what is happening inside of you. In seeing what lies within, you are able to experience the real sense of you.

9.

If intention does not come from a conscious place and is not in line with a higher sensitivity, then you open to all manner of distractions and potential corruption.

Blindly following another's belief goes against your innate nature. Learning how to experience the true self opens the doorway to changing reality. In forcing limiting structures on life, the true nature of living is not understood. Life becomes restricted by imposing form on creation that is forever moving and expanding. You become a bystander to life by being indifferent and impartial to what you see and do. If intention does not come from a conscious place and is not in line with a higher sensitivity, then you open to all manner of distractions and potential corruption. To live from the entirety of being you see this truth. In the direct experience of you, inner truth and belief grows. Here lies the inner knowing.

GUIDANCE   All restrictions come from what you believe you must be in the sight of others. To breathe is to know that peace cannot be given to you by anyone else. Living sovereignty is a natural state of being. To live a greater potential of you is to know that the most powerful force that resides within is in how you see yourself. This is because you create reality, so if you choose to believe that another person's ideal leads then that is what you follow. Begin by listening to what you believe and allow it to serve your higher good.

10.

To develop insight sensitively you must be aware of what you give attention to.

Where attention is placed becomes the focus. To develop insight sensitively you must be aware of what you give attention to. This means to answer to yourself, where you are the researcher and explorer of what feels right to you. By allowing the heart to lead, trust is reinstated in the creative life force that is the cradle of being. Vulnerability is no longer a daunting experience but the true guide to the way through. Coming to the edge of being and working through fear empowers truth where self-belief is strong. It is in the waking hour that the opportunity appears to create a living practice for realisation. Through dissolving the belief that suffering and pain are a permanent state, a truer life can be lived.

GUIDANCE   Listening to the way you speak is important. When you hear yourself speaking strongly about an issue notice whether that this is the true voice speaking. What is of value to you is most important. To follow blindly is to wear another one's robes for the wish to be like them. Inner truth cannot come like this. It comes when you sit with what you hear in you; to have the awareness to know whether this is real for you. To not hear your voice means you hide behind another. Try not to imagine what you should sound like but get to know what it is. To know what you feel and think about something matters. When you follow you sit as a passenger in life and not as the driver. To heal this pattern is to open into yourself and be in this inner reality. What touches you is of great value and if it is aligned to another's truth then this is a sharing but it is not what defines you, for this comes from you.

11.

That which feels wrong in you is needed to be seen to bring what feels right.

In reclaiming the true self, light is allowed to lead. From this point life has the potential to become simple and uncomplicated. Through the awakened heart can you be shown the path. The fragile nature of the soul can be seen in all feelings, thoughts and actions. That which feels wrong in you is needed to be seen to bring what feels right. This cannot happen when you follow blindly the interpretation of another. What is real resonates through the heart force. This is liberation where peace can grow. It is not by forcing change outside of you that brings lasting peace but when there is the entanglement of the chaos inside the soul. Integrity can be regained through this transformation and light reinstated.

GUIDANCE   Trusting instincts is not a complicated process or as difficult as you imagine. Instincts lie outside the mind and are more a felt sense. What makes you feel uneasy or unsure? When do you feel comfortable? This helps to orientate you to the part of you that is asking to open. To listen is to accept that when something does not feel right your higher intelligence is not trying to burden you. This is a genuine response that shows inner harmony is out of balance. Instead of ignoring the impulses that made you feel cautious, stop and become aware of it.

12.

You become trapped in making choices for approval and accept-ance and then reality is created out of what you believe others want from you and not from truth.

Understanding why the lack of responsibility exists so profoundly is essential to wellbeing. You become trapped in making choices for approval and acceptance and then reality is created out of what you believe others want from you and not from truth. In this reality it becomes necessary to let others guide. Living life through the translation of others cannot bring about truth. Buying into the collective experience is a heavy investment for you. To transform the level of powerlessness that exists you need to understand how it is created in the first place.

GUIDANCE   What this teaching is showing is to be aware of your inner process and allow this truth to lead. When you do this you stay true to encouraging your life with the essence of you and not a diluted version. When you lose touch with the inner realm you create a false self to fit in. This hides light and you show only a small part of who you are. Approval from others is not a blessing but makes you believe that you matter. You cannot sustain yourself in waiting for others approval.

13.

When you take responsibility you lead with truth and not fear.

Seeking the recognition of achievements to become accepted blinds you to light. This is the great escape that is created to ignore the pain in life. That which you run away from is created from you and so you can recreate it. The ulterior goal is to find respite from pain and so life is developed as an interface to seek safety and comfort. But this safety is limited for internal fear cannot be escaped or avoided. The external reality is the mirror for the internal world. When you take responsibility you lead with truth and not fear. From a place of fear external expression feels that it must be preserved at all cost. To live freely can't be achieved where fear exists for the shadows within creates the reality that you will live.

GUIDANCE   What is uncomfortable and painful within is hard to see. Sometimes respite is essential on our healing journey. But to only ever know yourself through hiding cannot grow light. Pain lives inside of you for good reason and not to overpower you. Life is conspiring to help you and this is its way of helping you realise that you are greater than what you can see. There lies a prayer in the heart that you will live to know yourself whole again and when you answer to its call you will find your way back.

What has been will be again.

Summary of Teachings

1. To come back to the true sense of being is a constant mission, for you have developed habits that search for answers outside of you.

2. In taking responsibility you seek to unblock what hides the heart from leading again.

3. You try to hold on to things that can never really be owned.

4. Connection that comes from within is giving and does not act out of the need for itself.

5. Through the arts, the heart is given permission to lead, having licence to dream.

6. It is not the shadow self that creates disempowerment but the pressure to achieve another's ideal.

7. Experiencing life through the feeling body allows the world to read what you need and in turn bring that to you.

8. Indifference appears when hope is lost but it is your unique soul journey that returns power and confidence to you.

9. If intention does not come from a conscious place and is not in line with a higher sensitivity, then you open to all manner of distractions and potential corruption.

10. To develop insight sensitively you must be aware of what you give attention to.

11. That which feels wrong in you is needed to be seen to bring what feels right.

12. You become trapped in making choices for approval and acceptance and then reality is created out of what you believe others want from you and not from truth.

13. When you take responsibility you lead with truth and not fear.

II
YOUR LIGHT

YOU CAN DECIDE TO BE VISIBLE AND LET LOVE IN

UNDERSTAND
that seeing all the shades within returns
integrity

LEARN
how you become lost when you reject parts
of you and accept others

BELIEVE
that the essence of love comes through
your sensitivity

1.

Nothing outside of you can deliver the highest wish if it does not exist within.

Out of fear comes the desire to seek control. Demanding breeds fear and defensiveness. When you control you force what you believe you should be and have. Through this you accept some parts of yourself and reject others. Nothing outside of you can deliver the highest wish if it does not exist within. Fragmentation follows for the true essence does not control or fix itself for it is ever flowing and unlimited. The path becomes a struggle when you become trapped in self-gaining. In the race with time with all its distractions it is easy to forget why you came. Life is a game of survival and the higher purpose is forgotten. To live the true essence, which is an unlimited state you must first see past the illusion driven from time. All wanting and seeking outside of you is for peace in the mind. Restrictions within cannot untether you, for sooner or later you feel stuck. Attachments come from the need to gain and the fear of losing. Giving inner responsibility away is detrimental to the potential of you.

GUIDANCE   When in touch with the abundant nature of being, this consciousness creates the reality outside of you. If your internal nature is restricted through passivity then the life you live will come from this sentiment. This is the principle of oneness. When harmony exists in you it will be created outside of you. The nature of healing shows this process very effectively. For example someone comes suffering from stress and anxiety because they experience not being good enough at their job. They find life a struggle as they continually feel dissatisfied. Trying to fix their external struggle by changing jobs or having less responsibility cannot change the imbalance that remains internally. What must change is how they see their self and the understanding of how anxiety and not feeling good enough came to be. To transform life outside of you is created from within you first. When you heal and resolve the imbalance within then life will effortlessly change to mirror your inner truth.

2.

When you are not visible, hidden, or corrupted in some way, then love turns into something else, you replace it with selectiveness and isolation.

Inner knowing comes when you accept all that you are. To become whole comes from inner exploration. To avoid yourself brings about further discord in life and to be free of this is to see yourself through pain. The creative power within functions unrestricted and all that is, is expressed through truth. The sentiment of your higher power is all giving. When you are not visible, hidden, or corrupted in some way, then love turns into something else, you replace it with selectiveness and isolation. What becomes alien to you is the creative life force within for it is now oppressed and controlled. Through this comes hesitation, for your fall weakens you. When you take responsibility of yourself there is the liberation of true power.

GUIDANCE   It is not easy to hear such words for many hide their selves away. The sadness of isolation can be seen everywhere. This is the tragic consequences of the loss of the true essence within. The question of where does love lie is not in the hands of authorities or of another but in the questioning of our own paths. To change this epidemic of loneliness that comes from being separate from the true self is when there is the courage to turn inwards and see what lies there without filters. When this happens you will find that your capacity to feel love grows and is the sustaining expression that does not depend on external circumstances.

3.

To live a limited existence stunts spiritual growth and light becomes dull

Fear generated in the heart restricts love and there is the struggle to give from the higher self. The heart cannot fully love because of suffering and in turn integrity becomes lost. To believe that you cannot catch yourself and live truth has de-spirited you. To have integrity is to have self-belief. You cheat yourself by seeking power through the easiest route outside of you but this cannot change the emptiness within. Making a choice to be visible in light is the greater challenge. To reinstall integrity you must not turn away from what exists in you for only through direct experience can you live the gift of the higher potential. To walk the way of your fire means you surrender the power game outside yourself. You do not fail anything by surrendering this external fight for it is illusionary and limiting. To live a limited existence stunts spiritual growth and light becomes dull. Healing occurs when in the journey to oneness you make the decision to see all of you. From pain you see the fight that traps you from light. To manage yourself is to face the discomfort within for it is the teacher that will provide you with what you are lacking.

GUIDANCE   The spiritual essence of you knows no boundaries and is the higher potential of being. To be spiritual has no form, for what is the living light needs no mediator for you to know it. Limitations come from that which oppresses truth. You can believe that you are held back by others who have power but this is what your inner frailty believes. To see what you have become is the path to retrieving power. When you see all the non-truths that lie in you then you will come to truth. To shine is to free the limitations you place on yourself.

4.

Truth does not live in the pursuit of affirmation from another but in realising light.

You are hesitant to see yourself naked and live the belief of light that is the divine within. You keep hidden from life because you fear the restrictions that are in you. Your fall is not for punishment, to make you feel shame and further grief. To forgive is the release of the illusion that keeps you separate from the oneness state. To accept vulnerability in you with love is to realise that failure does not exist. You fear the judgement of yourself and punish your being. Truth does not live in the pursuit of affirmation from another but in realising light. Light expresses itself in its unique way. In surrendering there can be another way of living. When you find alignment to the true state the song of your fire becomes the seed to the higher path. To realise truth raises you out of the darkness of pain.

GUIDANCE When self-belief wanes to know that you possess great power and light becomes full of doubt. Even when you say that you will not hide yourself beneath the words you remain nervous to the path. It is not the potential of reaching this goal that people fear for many have become experts at goal setting. What is feared is placing this goal to one side and learning about the nervousness that remains inside of you. We trick ourselves in the expectation of what will come and get lost in the fantasy of what may be. Realisation is a state of being that has no future or past for it is all that exists in this moment. What you are in the here and now matters and this is living light.

5.

Through seeing every shade of you from the darkest to the lightest parts is of great value.

To be visible is to be seen and to see all your colours. When able to radiate from truth, light resonates strongly. Through seeing every shade of you from the darkest to the lightest parts is of great value. This spectrum is vast in being but needs understanding in order to free the higher potential. What is truth will guide you to light. As soon as you become hidden, restricted and fragmented what is light becomes darker and what is seen is now unseen. What remains is pain. When something is hidden then it needs to be kept safe. You seek protection and sadness comes out of the struggle of knowing you have lost a part of yourself. Pain and the pursuit of external power then becomes the reality of your pursuits. When there is a barrier to the heart opening, then you seek another to carry you to feel complete. To be complete is freedom where you do not seek for anything.

GUIDANCE   We experience a reality of division all the time. We label and attach negative and positive beliefs about the shades of the self. Living openly moves beyond these restrictions, and reinstates a flow where you are not held back but can see the true value of all parts of yourself. In healing it can feel painful to realise how far you have come from that which feels free. Pain recedes when you don't give up. No one can tell you how long this will take, as each person's path is perfect for what they need to learn. What is known is with perseverance and courage you can and will come to completion.

6.

The light of being knows its way home, for it is without discord and lives for the highest good.

Every moment there is a choice, either to create from what is real or to give in to fear. To live free, courage from the heart needs to open. This opening allows for the truest response to the environment. Your sensitivity acts as a sense organ that opens the doorway to liberate you from fear. The light of being knows its way home, for it is without discord and lives for the highest good. It causes itself and others no harm. This knowledge remains distant and is a forgotten truth. Resolve of pain when in light becomes instantaneous, for it exists free from limitations. To de-clutter distraction to self-empowerment is to learn the principles of awareness and observation of the self. To see that the truth of life does not need to be given or attained from another but to know that this lies within the self already. You know what to believe in and what not to, what the right path is and what is not for you. This knowing comes in direct experience of what is authentic for you.

GUIDANCE   Trust in yourself, inner knowing and self-belief come from your true state. To trust within is to realise that the internal response you have to the world around you is real for you. The reason this is not easy to do is because you desperately want to believe that you are something else and want to mould yourself to suit a false image that you have. To open to parts of you that come from truth is to accept what you see. In this moment give value to your inner knowing. Let go of attaching to the way you believe you should be because until you do you cannot return belief in yourself.

7.

The higher task calls the inner reality to be lived fully with no borders to truth.

Without oneness you will continue to seek for something. Through endless interpretations to living a happy and peaceful life you avoid pain. Polarity exists in life because this polarity exists within. The higher search is for the oneness state where you are complete, whole and empowered, where life's illusions are no longer. In the return to light is the knowing of freedom where a higher reality is understood. The mission of coming into the world is to free from fear and live in union. The journey to light is to forgive yourself that fear is in you. In surrendering you know that you create your destiny and what you are matters. The higher task calls the inner reality to be lived fully and with no borders to truth. To join into the higher ground is found through healing from discord and freeing from what ties you. Within the sovereign state you do not need anything but to create from oneness.

GUIDANCE   When you can hear truth and then are able to make changes in life this often means that you have travelled far to strengthening the core of the self already. This may have come from life times of healing or developing your inner knowing. When you experience that you have many hurdles to cross within then try to refrain from comparing yourself to another. In comparing you bring doubt into life and yet there is no value for you doing this. To accept where you are is humility for you are in the right place for you. Many become lost in resentment and bitterness and consume their self with pain of their hardship. You have come to where you are not by some accident or trickery but by the choices that you have co-created over life times. Taking responsibility of who you are now is to accept yourself.

8.

It is those that challenge fear and walk their truth that create through the higher self and live the life of empowerment.

You seek happiness outside yourself. Such seeking brings a second hand truth where you quickly become lost to pain and fear. Through this comes a fight for fear has become an enemy. Fear is a much needed process to signal to you that something needs attention for its role is helping prepare you. In fear you become alert, heightened and ready for what is to come. Fear is the alarm bell that shows you that you need to go within. Beyond fear you surrender to the truth of what you feel. What is in the heart requires itself to be seen and made visible. The more you are able to see within the more you are able to be with love. You may need help with this but the wish to go there has to be your intention. Surpassing the illusion of fear you come to light. To come out of the light of fire is to be with peace, to know that the power is within and is the natural state. It is those that challenge fear and walk their truth that create through the higher self and live the life of empowerment.

GUIDANCE   Every inner fear that people face transforms their reality. Why? Coming into the darkness of the void returns a part of your integrity and humbles you. This allows you to see that even in a fragile state you can climb a great mountain. This experience cannot be given to you by another but only when you feel this do you hold the subtlety and strength of the power within you. It is through the opening of the soul and becoming all that you are do you know who you are.

9.

The collective corruption inflicts shame and this weakens you.

You choose to give power away or keep it. What is true from the heart is pure in intention and will seek to be shared for there are no shadows created from it. The influence of the external world is made to feel important. From this you are led. What is then hidden from within is long forgotten. Life becomes filled with the need for protection on all levels of being. Such a reality is ailing and has brought madness into the world. The healing process is the understanding of the unease of life and how you become caught in struggle. In despair you become lost to shame in forgetting the truth within and seek to punish yourself. What waits in you is light, for this truth is always there where shame does not exist. The collective corruption inflicts shame and weakens you. In the strength of truth you reverse this reality of life. Instead of being caught in the flames of pain you are asked to take responsibility of all that you are and find the higher power. When there is disempowerment then you choose to avoid pain.

GUIDANCE   The higher teachings show that no other has authority to bring you shame for this comes from a corrupt place. Though it is now part of the greater culture it does not mean that it is a truth. What you believe in has the greatest impact in you and if you decide to believe that shame is of value then this is what you create. That which is of light will always seek to lift you and not condemn. What is true will find a way to empower you through pain and not punish you. This knowing comes from light.

10.

The true state of being is replaced with tyranny and in such conflict it is hard to accept imperfection.

The way of empowerment is to make yourself visible. To hide no parts is to live tenderness, for all is accepted and all welcomed. You are not responsible for how others see you. The higher wish is to feel what you are and to not hide what is true to you. The true state is replaced with tyranny and in such conflict it is hard to accept imperfection. Light lives to be expressed through its unlimited self but judgement and comparison keeps you trapped. When there is care in you this brings the tenderness needed for the path of self-realisation. Truth is formed by the direct seeing of this unshakable and self-sustaining power. This is wished for in the higher self, to join in love.

GUIDANCE   Discovering the spectrums that exist in you is never ending. A myth that you want to believe is that there is a magical solution to everything and everything must come to some conclusion. Life is an endless journey of discovery, even when you are free of fear you are only beginning the greater journey. You don't just stop, you are eternal. Whether you experience good or bad feeling, live a happy or sad life you will carry on, there is no end. What this teaching shows is that you put off facing fear in the hope that you will not be confronted and remain living a safe and perfect life. To live imperfectly is your true state. Life on earth gives you the opportunity to know the wonder of you and set you free.

11.

Personal struggle forces you to feel truth.

What is being asked of you is to fight the battle of righting the wrongs that have been sown over lifetimes. The wish to become visible again lays heavy in the heart for you become used to hiding. You feel that facing the shadow is too much to carry. Self-belief comes out of truth alone and when this leads fear will diminish. In lifetimes of pain comes the seed of hate where suffering takes over. Personal struggle forces you to feel truth. It does this for it asks you to breathe into light. The fears within are shallow compared to the power of the true self. This is the leap of faith that life is encouraging you to take. You become the master and realise the purpose of what you came for. Love waits for you when you are ready to open to all that you are.

GUIDANCE   You may get lost in trying to find the reasons why misfortune happens to you. People fear being a bad person and the loss of acceptance from others. The search for this outside comes because of the lack of faith that exists within the potential of you. If you believe that you need saving then you encourage discord in life to persist. Love knows no hierarchy for it is one with all. You are the saint, the deliverer and the saviour. Your pain is what is real for you and that is what you need to see to develop the higher truth. If this was taken away from you then you will not know your light. To have compassion for each other's journey is the beauty in life. Each of us has the opportunity to go deeper and know more. In doing this for our self we help each other.

12.

The challenge in life is to remember the higher task and to tackle the depths of grief and sorrow that remains the obstacle to empowerment.

The stream of life that you are accustomed to brings endless distractions. The challenge is to remember the higher task and to tackle the depths of grief and sorrow that remains the obstacle to empowerment. When love enters that which is created is lived out of the higher self. Live truth and it will bring about a power that will create an unshakable belief where you do not forget who you are. From oneness all of sorrow and the mayhem that is cast in the depths of you can be processed effortlessly. It is through the creative power that you find the strength to heal yourself and to honour this freedom. All that remains is to know what you come with and align to this higher truth. For this to manifest begins by mastering fear.

GUIDANCE   No one can rescue you from the sorrow that you feel for this originated from the moment you separated from the oneness state and is the original wound. Peace comes when you come to the eye of the storm within you. Grief remains in you when you are still to realise yourself. To live peace in you, you must live the chaos until all that remains is peace. To be proactive in remembering how to be real is important as many things in life do not come out of this light but from discord. Fill your life with positivity, with ideas and constructs that are life giving and believe in the greatness of you. Read, listen or be with those who promote this. The stream of life that is of light becomes greater when everyone takes responsibility for their own shining.

13.

Freedom lies in the knowing that you can decide to make yourself visible again and let love in.

To surrender to all that you are brings self-realisation. To decide what is real inside of you gives you power and brings balance within. Freedom lies in the knowing that you can decide to make yourself visible again and let love in. This is how you begin the unfolding to the true state of being. Knowing the self is to remember how you came to be as you are. You do not have to be stuck in the struggle of pain but to believe in the boundless state of love that asks to be realised by you.

GUIDANCE   Handling yourself is a careful task. Imagine a child that is attempting to do something that is difficult and at the very first hurdle they break down in tears and say they can't do it. Each time you come to what feels like a hurdle you are facing a negative belief within. To feel unconfident has many layers to it. You will open and close yourself, you will attempt to move into the unknown and then return to the safety of the known. This dance is part of the healing and releasing process. Just because you have not done what you had hoped, or was expected of you, do not believe you have done nothing. Each time you remember to look within you come closer to the true self. This path will test you for what you ask for is light and so to see it you may have to pass through darkness. Your story is yours alone and it is the celebration of you in all colours. When you feel like giving up remind yourself to go carefully.

Summary of Teachings

1. Nothing outside of you can deliver the highest wish if it does not exist within.

2. When you are not visible, hidden, or corrupted in some way, then love turns into something else, you replace it with selectiveness and isolation.

3. To live a limited existence stunts spiritual growth and light becomes dull.

4. Truth does not live in the pursuit of affirmation from another but in realising light.

5. Through seeing every shade of you from the darkest to the lightest parts is of great value.

6. The light of being knows its way home, for it is without discord and lives for the highest good.

7. The higher task calls the inner reality to be lived fully with no borders to truth.

8. It is those that challenge fear and walk their truth that create through the higher self and live the life of empowerment.

9. The collective corruption inflicts shame and this weakens you.

10. The true state of being is replaced with tyranny and in such conflict it is hard to accept imperfection.

11. Personal struggle forces you to feel truth.

12. The challenge in life is to remember the higher task and to tackle the depths of grief and sorrow that remains the obstacle to empowerment.

13. Freedom lies in the knowing that you can decide to make yourself visible again and let love in.

WHEN VULNERABLE TREAD SLOWLY

UNDERSTAND
that vulnerability is not a weakness for it brings peace

LEARN
how through frailty you gain humility

BELIEVE
you can steer the way when you feel vulnerable

1.

*You have protected yourself because you feel you have good
reason to and not because you are weak.*

With courage show the world what you hold for in truth
lays your power. You get used to showing some parts of you
and hiding others. You filter what you want others to see and
what you don't. To live life this way breeds fragmentation
and borders within. This is created from fear inside of you.
The true expression lives without borders and has no need to
hide any parts of its self. In a powerless state you experience
sorrow to what you have now become. When you surrender
to truth then self-belief can be. When this place is unfamiliar
then the unknown scares you. To walk this path you must
go slowly and not rush. You have protected yourself because
you feel you have good reason too and not because you are
weak. Emotions and thoughts are powerful and affect you to a
profound level for they are the reality you live. To free the fire
within is a careful task for you are wary of getting burnt. To
awaken that which is Holy comes from the higher sensitivity
of being. You may not experience this sensitivity and may feel
overwhelmed at the prospect of feeling too much. To open is
to re-learn to trust yourself and awaken this potential. This is
the figuring out of knowing the love within. To see this you
need space and tenderness for easily you feel overshadowed.

GUIDANCE   There lies a higher intelligence that knows how
to look after you. Often it works through your subconscious
and finds the solution to anything that you may feel could
harm you. The resilience of human nature is vast in surviving

powerful and intense experiences. In the rush to heal ourselves and go quickly through anything that feels uncomfortable the power of healing is overlooked. To heal cannot be about ticking a box, there is no magical pill for you to swallow to make everything go away. Much of my work is helping people to see that there are many layers to healing and to be present in it, you have to slow down. It may feel like you are not in control within it but it is when you let go are you able to feel release. Emotion is energy, it is not some transparent figment of your imagination and this is why it can feel big. These teachings show you that having the courage to face the discomfort is the higher way but you must do it at the pace that's right for you. To unpack years of holding on to discord would harm you more if you force yourself to face pain too quickly. When you feel overwhelmed and highly anxious stop for this may be the time to reach out for support.

2.

You are learning to get used to a vulnerable state for it feels a heightened experience which you are not used too.

To be vulnerable is to see what is real and to experience all that it is showing you. You forget this task when you become lost in the wanting of what is outside of you. When faced with the realness of being it can feel intense for it comes with the power of truth. When you have not lived this way for so long this can feel an unfamiliar terrain. You struggle to have self-belief because internal shadows bring you down. To have direct experience of what you come with holds meaning for you. Freeing pain allows you to feel into vulnerability for this is what you fear doing. You fear it because you are used to hiding and feel exposed in this unfamiliar territory. This is a challenge to move through this process and open at the same time. You can do this with support and kindness so that you can go at the pace that you are comfortable with. Knowing that you have spent maybe lifetimes running away from this shows that by moving carefully you succeed to change the experience of yourself. You are learning to get used to a vulnerable state for it feels a heightened experience which you are not used too. The vulnerable state is the doorway that brings you towards freedom in the heart.

GUIDANCE   When you have to experience intense feelings that either scare you or are unfamiliar you can go through a forced opening. For example when working with people in order to elevate their sensitivity they experience their self in a higher state. This experience moves them to a tender, careful place where they sense their self much more. This is a pleasant experience and this careful opening feels good. When you have to experience intense pain or emotion the body energetically responds in the same way. Even in an unpleasant experience you are raised to a higher place but it is your pain that creates the bridge to going higher. In either case whether it is a forced or a careful opening, this unfamiliar experience needs to be integrated slowly. To get used to a different expression of you takes time and energy to adapt to.

3.

To accept yourself in frailty is to have humility and in this state
you experience the power of grace.

That which is the Holy is derived when you attain freedom
within and live without limitations. To feel vulnerability is a
necessary state to open. You are used to living out of a hard
place and experiencing lower energies. To go slowly is to be
careful. For in the vastness of the self lies many traps and it is
this fear that you must pass. Being vulnerable makes you feel
weak but in truth you feel your humanness. To feel tenderness
is the same essence as praying. To accept yourself in frailty is
to have humility and in this state you experience the power
of grace. This incredible gift of acceptance is what helps you
face the diversity of pain. From this place you are able to
allow truth to be what it needs to be. To feel exposed, is to
not hold back but witness who you become in it. In opening, the higher self waits to reveal its reality. This place feels
frightening and so you shut down for protection. It's often
not until someone has the sensitivity to see their frailty that
they can ask for help. Facing your fear with acceptance and
not judgement, shame or blaming enables you to receive the
help you need.

GUIDANCE   To experience hardness is to be distant in the
world, where the heart is not leading brings coldness into life.
You can fool yourself that being cold and hard is a valued
trait for it elevates you and brings you confidence with an
aggressive surety. This discord fuels a careless way of being
and is why feeling exposed to your vulnerability feels unsafe as

others see you as weak or childish. Humility cuts through all power struggles and is the power of truth. To live with grace is to know strength that comes with tenderness and never aggression.

4.

To feel the world from the heart is to understand care.

When you are no longer separated from the natural state then a truer essence of love is felt. When the heart is no longer shut off or hidden you feel love. You cannot really describe this love for it has no borders; it is free from corruption and is unconditional. The essence of love cannot be reasoned; it must be felt and so cannot be reached by functioning from the mind alone. To feel the world from the heart is to understand care. Struggle is created within from the avoidance of pain and so to move out of this reality you return by being led by the heart. When the heart is open and is allowed to feel all the spectrum of its self you have the possibility to reach love and create meaning. When there is fear in the heart there is restriction and the internal culture becomes bound by subtle fears. Out of self-preservation life becomes starved of what is truly needed and here grows the poverty in life. The inner realm is dictated by feelings and thoughts and so to master this reality you begin to know how to nurture and grow these faculties consciously. Seeing what you have become requires you to slow down, to learn awareness practices that give space and compassion for the internal chaos.

GUIDANCE   When you live with fear it is hard to understand what it is like not to have this. This is why it is important to make your exploration a direct experience. You cannot learn this by text alone; it has to be your experience of it that changes the internal perspective. All the divisions created in life have spread from the existence of fear. To become a universal being is to know no borders within. Fear separates, divides and seeks to control. To open to a new way of being is to heal that which the heart carries so that you can reconnect with what has meaning for you.

5.

You cannot show yourself when you are lost in the fight for power outside of you.

When vulnerable you become heightened and come closer to the potential of hearing the true voice that leads you to the Holy within. To find this path realises the higher aspect of you. You cannot show yourself when you are lost in the fight for power outside of you. You are learning to remember and awaken that which is Holy within. When you fear vulnerability you fear the power of the true self. You fear being the true creator of reality with years or lifetimes of settling with indifference and following another's wish. It is through this fall that brings the chance to remember how to create yourself again, to free out of the discord of the past and to not be tied to anything. To believe in light is to surrender to what is real inside of you and not to battle against it.

GUIDANCE   In the struggle for power is the rise of tyranny in life. All power games lose you to corruption. To want to overcome another in the gain for personal power brings darkness into the world. You may believe that there is no other way to empower yourself but in truth it is the fear within you that frightens you the most. You are called to let go of the illusion of ever winning an external fight for it lay's heavy in the heart and only binds you further to a powerless state. No reward, prestige, robe or title can give you the sustaining power which you search for.

6.

Vulnerability is invoked when you lift the veil of what remains hidden to you.

Fear forces you to acquire strength externally. You struggle to want to hold on to that which you do not feel you have. Surrendering is not giving up it is the opening to all that you are. You need courage to face fear and in opening you begin to take back power. To safely open to vulnerability helps you face the deepest fears. Vulnerability is invoked when you lift the veil of what remains hidden to you. Resistance to seeing the shadow parts of you feels as if they could disempower or weaken you further. This is part of the karmic cycle that you are trying to break. Opening to feeling what you have become lays the potential to overcome the wound that you are tied to. To continue to carry karma makes the spirit of you heavy. You see vulnerability as weak but it emanates from a tender part in your being. In a more harshly dominated world you mistake vulnerability for weakness because you forget what peace is. From a place of peace you naturally go slowly and look after all. Many will not fully understand this for they do not know peace. To open is to be free.

GUIDANCE   For something to be exposed there needs to be something hidden. Therefore when something is not hidden we are able to relax and live our lives with ease. This is sensitive because it's been necessary for you to close off these parts or you would not have done it. This very act is challenging how you see yourself and this feels unsafe without going carefully. When someone holds a conscious healing space for you it can give you the safety net that you need to open and learn about yourself. Feeling vulnerable is not comfortable but it does not mean you can't move through it. Life is full of many discomforts where you choose to not be part of. To feel the discomfort of yourself is an absolutely necessary step to experiencing what is authentic and real in you.

7.

To stay safe within discord is no safety.

You choose the path you lead. Where there is corruption then there are blocks to feeling safe to showing vulnerability. You do not want to go to a place that feels unsafe no matter who tells you. To stay safe in discord is no safety. That which cannot be resolved within will continue to affect you until you heal. To avoid or runaway only buys you time but cannot solve suffering. To surrender is to walk with fear and break the illusion that tries to keep you in a false sense of safety. To be cast from wholeness within is to re-learn the way of your truth before you can harvest inner light.

GUIDANCE   It is an illusion to believe that you have a safe internal culture when you try to escape fear. The sensitivity of life knows what you carry and this is what continues to create the life you lead. You get used to a certain level of safety in the world that keeps you distant. Agitation, worry, stress and subtle addictions are all signs to show that you do not feel truly safe. To wake up from helplessness is to learn about what you carry. Opening comes in so many ways and you are able to find the way that works for you. All paths that encourage awareness, opening, careful practice, tenderness and self-belief help you and do not disempower. Beginning this and persevering changes the reality you live.

8.

The state of vulnerability is the perfect place to reach the higher potential for it gives you access to fear.

The state of vulnerability is the perfect place to reach the higher potential for it gives you access to fear. Because of the intensity that you may experience in the inner world, go slowly. Having kindness to yourself and having the right support when exploring pain is essential for well-being. Even through discomfort you can be held from loved ones, friends, healers or carers. When you live separated from the true state you cannot show all of yourself. To be awakened in living is to be real, for you weaken what is real when you follow another. To drive yourself is the destiny to the higher potential.

GUIDANCE   To resist feeling vulnerable is the norm, people will distract their self to escape it. It is not liked because it feels exposing and you don't feel relaxed in it. But it is the precursor to seeing a fear in you. This is a necessary state and it is preparing your sensitivity of seeing. Fear masks truth and in truth lays the potential to grow to wholeness. Without opening you cannot experience what matters to you, what moves you and in turn what lies as the higher teaching. To dull sensitivity cannot help free you but acts as a depressant. To walk into the void of yourself you have to let go. Opening may not seem easy and seeking those who understand how to navigate this terrain can help.

9.

When the heart suffers hardship it wishes to seek resolve.

To live in an integrated way comes from what is created out of meaning. This becomes the guiding truth and principle that leads you forward. To experience unsettled feelings within is the showing that a healing process is needed. Fear wants to control this process and so carries anticipation of what may lie ahead and tries to avoid it at all cost. To be lost in avoidance renders you powerless. Looking to another to suppress pain weakens you. Acceptance of what lies within is the first step away from pain. When the heart suffers hardship it wishes to seek resolve. Without resolve you remain stuck until internal balance is returned. The true purpose of why you came is to face this challenge head on for this has the greatest meaning for you. From personal truth you shine. To shine is to be clear, open and have the courage to love freely especially yourself. In the divine self you are sacred. All is hallowed, clear and justified. This is the intimacy of life.

GUIDANCE   The heart is a memory bank that holds unresolved issues from all you have ever experienced. What has the most meaning to you remains with you over lifetimes and this includes the lighter parts too. Clearing the way of what burdens the heart is a great service to all. What you carry has come out of the unique expression of your personal journey. For each of us there are magnificent tales to be told. In the telling of this story comes self-belief. Resolve comes in the complete knowing of how you came to be who you are. This lifts the burden and brings the healing you need to let go. Release plays a significant part in healing for then you start harvest truth.

10.

No one can awaken you; you must wish to figure this out
for yourself.

Peace is not separate from the pain of life for they are often close companions. When you accept the shadow parts then that which lies beyond is the realisation of hope. Going slowly allows your nature to unfold in freeing itself from that which it is not. Happiness and strength lies in showing for here is meaning. It is when you shine that you are able to overcome suffering more. To grow into the wish of the true self is found in the showing of all you are. No one can awaken you; you must wish to figure this out for yourself. No one can bring you what is real as this can only be delivered out of you. Happiness lies in the Holy for that is what is connected to an unlimited creative force.

GUIDANCE   Living a spiritual path is unique for everyone. No one has the same experience regardless of what spiritual expression you follow the interpretation of its meaning is yours alone. To want conformity breeds control. A spiritual path gives life when it is integrated throughout the whole of you. That which is Holy, Sacred and Divine is within you and you are not separate from it. If external acts of devotion do not come from the heart then it is meaningless for you, you must feel the devotion in you for it to be of service outside of you.

11.

To create out of the higher fire is to surrender and give value to all that makes you feel vulnerable.

What blocks you from being vulnerable is when there is fixation on pain and fear. You become stuck, you feel there is no way out and in despair you cannot do anything. In the expectation that you must find a way out you become powerless. You are not stuck but rather need to focus your attention and strength to face fear. If you believe you can't then you may need to ask for help. This is not to follow someone blindly but to be supported with a sincere wish to take responsibility. To not forget to open leads you to succeed in the negation of suffering. To create out of the higher fire is to surrender and give the value to all that makes you feel vulnerable. In this you train to live from the heart. You must go slowly because there are new skills to learn. You use these skills to awaken the will to the true self.

GUIDANCE   These teachings make you feel into a new way of being. This mirrors the extreme way in which the collective has strayed from higher living. There are cultures that understand this way of living more than others, who place forgiveness and understanding ahead of punishment and persecution. What is the loudest message is to learn to strike a balance to living the parts of you that have been hidden and unaccepted. You are being called to give attention to the internal world, to realise that what you seek outside so earnestly is found in the experience of you.

12.

To see truth in sorrow is to open to love.

Life is given to create more life. When you forget who you are then you see only pain. Within is the longing to awaken that which grieves for itself. To follow the higher wish is to bring freedom from within and light the way. Behind each pain lays the renewal of life that is hope. You first must open to reveal the strength of truth to find that which is wisdom. You battle for power, the power outside and inside yourself.

In you is the potential to live from the heart again. To see truth in sorrow is to open to love. Until grief comes you mask truth and can live a lie. The path of truth is in fear where you are given the opportunity to forgive yourself. With healing and surrendering to what is real comes the showing of the beauty of light and that is the tenderness of joy.

GUIDANCE   Relief and joy comes from release. Every time you battle to hold back your sadness you miss the opportunity to come to peace. Without release where does sadness go? It remains in the heart hidden and pushed down. This affects the quality of experiencing the whole of yourself. Love is peace, the tenderness that comes when you surrender the fight of holding back pain. To find out how to live the true self is to open and free all that you are. The unknown is your teacher without it you cannot grow light.

13.

The heart becomes strong when it surrenders to the creative force within, for all answers are revealed to you.

Following others teaches you to not consider what lies within. You must go slowly to change this reality for it has been a long time since empowerment was created from within. To take responsibility is to carry everything that you have become. You can create reality and deliver the dream within the heart. The heart becomes strong when it surrenders to the creative force, for all answers are revealed to you. Making a choice to follow the goodness of light is what you are learning to do. Joy is its highest expression. Your fall is the battle to open the heart with care again.

GUIDANCE   You are not empty. In the fear of facing impending loneliness is the fantasy that nothing exists, that you are void of life. You are created out of the life giving forces of creation, this is you. When all the noise of the soul quietens you experience a different way of being. This way cannot be likened to the life you have lived, for all that you have known does not grow this potential. Harnessing the inner faculties of knowing through the senses begins to awaken another stream of life that you have been distracted from. The inner world is as vast as the universe and when you free all that weigh's you down you will begin to live interconnected where life has the possibility to breathe a higher light.

Summary of Teachings

1. You have protected yourself because you feel you have good reason too and not because you are weak.

2. You are learning to get used to a vulnerable state for it feels a heightened experience which you are not used too.

3. To accept yourself in frailty is to have humility and in this state you experience the power of grace.

4. To feel the world from the heart is to understand care.

5. You cannot show yourself when you are lost in the fight for power outside of you.

6. Vulnerability is invoked when you lift the veil of what remains hidden to you.

7. To stay safe within discord is no safety.

8. The state of vulnerability is the perfect place to reach the higher potential for it gives you access to fear.

9. When the heart suffers hardship it wishes to seek resolve.

10. No one can awaken you; you must wish to figure this out for yourself.

11. To create out of the higher fire is to surrender and give value to all that makes you feel vulnerable.

12. To see truth in sorrow is to open to love.

13. The heart becomes strong when it surrenders to the creative force within, for all answers are revealed to you.

HEALING GRIEF

UNDERSTAND
that through vulnerability you find yourself

LEARN
to follow light to create the world you want
to live in

BELIEVE
that it is only you that holds yourself back

1.

Sorrow runs deep within not because it is part of the
natural state of being but because of the separation from
oneness within.

To some degree or other you will experience intense sorrow, whether it is from pain or from the loss of another. Sorrow runs deep not because it is part of the natural state of being but because of the separation from oneness within. In truth you lay beyond all sorrow. Grief exists to help refine you and when honoured can lighten the burden of fear. To honour this natural process you take down the masks that you have been hiding behind and open. This sensitivity is the higher self that is allowed to be part of you, unrestricted and freely flowing. When you run away from this internal dying process you fall further away from the opportunity to awaken the higher aspect of you. If fear exists then it is there to strengthen you with the aim of retrieving a true power. You can give many reasons why pain exists but grief lives in you to help you surrender and come to realisation. To feel helpless to pain you are caught in managing, seeking relief, escaping and playing external games to avoid what is in you. You remain in struggle until you face the fear that you are running away from.

GUIDANCE   Intense emotion exists because it has to and not because it is a cruel infliction on you. People lose their self in how they have suffered at the hands of an awful event or people. This response seeks for justice, someone to blame or to prove wrong. The higher teaching shows that you are as responsible for the reality of pain inside of you as those who have been part of it. Understand that to blame another allows for no growth on either part. What is necessary and gives life is for each one to take responsibility of their pain. Without this process you will not forgive and remain trapped in creating further discord.

2.

The sadness that emanates through grief is the consequence of losing trust and falling to the shame of what you have become.

Without fear restricting, you are free to surrender to the creative life force and to love unconditionally. You become the master from trusting within. The sadness that emanates through grief is the consequence of losing trust and falling to the shame of what you have become. But shame keeps you stuck and prevents you from moving forward. To lose yourself in shame helps no one and only fuels a culture of punishment. This is counteractive to what is truth within. To surrender to the process of grief can help you to catch yourself in the fall, to empower you but never to punish. To live with pain exists because you have not mastered your reality free. Such a freedom comes when you live without borders and challenge yourself to open to what really lives beyond grief. When you strengthen the heart this allows you to remain open through pain. Living from the heart you loosen the grip of control that comes out of a time bound reality bred from fear. With control you live for targets and become burdened. For life to be transformed from pain to love, you seek to move into the higher aspect and take responsibility for what you carry.

GUIDANCE   Many healing truths remain unknown because few people want to hear them. To go deeper in healing is often someone's last resort for they have tried everything and their pain has not gone away. Main stream approaches try to tackle pain by numbing the senses and so hope for the best in maintaining some level of well-being. We are multi-dimensional sentient beings and to be in health we must find balance in all parts of our being. To have imbalance is because you need it at some higher level. The more you can bring awareness to the sensitivity within you actively open and start to change the reality of resistance.

3.

To be honest in how you really feel, to accept fear breeds no further discord inside but frees you into a higher state.

Showing is essential for personal care to exist in the world. To realise this, you walk naked, even when you feel alienated to speak truth. The innate being of you is to become all that it needs to be. It is honoured when free from discord that limits its life force from growing. To show yourself is to not break the trust within. By doing this you come to self-belief and the realisation of truth becomes part of life. When you remain hidden you hide power. To be honest in how you really feel, to accept fear breeds no further discord inside but frees you into a higher state. You have invested a lot in trying to avoid vulnerability and now it is hard to see the way. We live in a culture that has become hard, built on foundations where the heart has been closed from carrying much pain. By releasing emotion you surrender to truth even though it can feel you hurt more, this will pass.

GUIDANCE   Release comes in the moment that you are honest to yourself. It sounds so simple. Imagine that for the next few minutes you will decide to share everything that is going on inside of you. What fills your thoughts? Let yourself feel free to see what you are in this moment, do you reveal something to yourself? To check in with yourself is a valuable practice because you can get so used to not seeing all parts of you. When you do this you are breaking the habit of keeping things hidden from yourself.

4.

The heart feels broken but it is not, in truth it is you opening through the expansion of yourself.

When the heart opens through grief there lays the feeling to the Holy. To allow grief to be you are forced to detach from the external world. This is the body bringing you to where you need to be to honour it. Grief is the potential to move you to light. The power of such a release of emotions opens the heart; this is the letting go process. The heart feels broken but it is not, in truth it is you opening through the expansion of yourself. To be fully human is to show the true way of being. When you live by outside formalities then you become trapped by time or place and cannot truly listen to what moves you from within. You are learning to follow the heart. In opening you remember that which is forgotten. The choice is to live what is lying in the prayer of the heart and to follow this truth that wishes to be realised. In seeing the ways in which the intensities of pain and sorrow affects you, the internal battle that it draws to the surface finds relief. These feelings have always been within and have waited for this time to unburden you. To not hide this struggle is to shine a higher state into life. To be conscious is to be awake to all that you feel. When you live in oneness life can be lived through the Holy. When the inner voice is listened to then trust is cast into being.

GUIDANCE   When I hear the expression to have a broken heart I compare it to the actual state that people go through in healing. Often when you open there is a sense of an ache in the heart, powerful intense feelings can rise. The heart does not break, creating further suffering but grows. Energetically the heart is stretching open as its capacity to feel deepens and so in sorrow the heart is going through growing pains until it reaches a place where the emotions are stable again. To expand into your being is of great service to you. To imagine the heart breaking defeats the capacity for recovery. Looking after the fragile nature of the soul is to understand the heart force and value the true potential of its strength.

5.

When life's processes of struggle and healing present them-selves, you are forced to the core of you.

Through grief you come to the core of longing. This is the higher wish that waits to be realised. When you live for external pursuit the higher wish becomes shut off. Life is asking you not to shut off what you long for but to have hope through grief and it will teach you. The task is the realisation of the true self and the knowing of all you are. When life's processes of struggle and healing present themselves, you are forced to the core of you. The release of emotion is the flow that frees the heart. It asks you to not forget this aspect, to not cast it away in fear and believe it to be futile but to remember that here lays truth and meaning. Yes you hurt. It hurts because you forget why grief exists in the first place. It came from the original pain of separating from the oneness state. On this path to freedom of the self is learning how to live whole again.

GUIDANCE   It becomes a norm to not live from the very centre of being. You remain detached from within and long to succeed in the outer world. The memory of the healing process lies uncomfortably because you see it as a down fall, something that should not have to happen. You seek happiness and love externally in the hope that you find fulfilment. To come to resolve within is peace. Your story is a great story to be told and the teaching of it to be gleaned in celebration. Encouraging these stories to be told is of great value to us. Replenishing the way we see healing is essential for the potential of spiritual growth and evolution.

6.

We are affected profoundly when we experience an external bereavement and the grief is similar to the internal dying process of the self-image.

We are affected profoundly when we experience an external bereavement and the grief is similar to the internal dying process of the self-image. When you hold on to pain and not let go you become shut to what is real and the potential of the inner fire. Your fire comes out of the powerful forces within that become aligned when fear does not restrict you. Without the discord of pain you move towards what you came for, to live into supreme consciousness. Holding on cannot help you to harness the powers that lie beyond grieving and to the greater potential of you. You have the opportunity to lift higher when you honour grief. In life learning to create and re-create yourself, to be the master of reality is what you are here for but this cannot be done when you hold on. What creates reality comes from intention and what you believe in. When you cannot access truth then the foundation of belief is found through external sources.

GUIDANCE   Rarely do people welcome the healing process. Your attention and energy is essential to face internal struggle. It often comes as a big surprise that the process takes so much out of you. It does this because for so long you have invested heavily in a way of being and are used to comfort even if it does not serve you or hold you back. To let go you may have to face a spectrum of emotion that comes with grief, anger, sorrow, despair or loneliness. But when you go through this storm there lays peace. It comes when you have understood yourself enough to let go.

7.

The level of fear or light determines the intensity of grief that you experience.

When facing the death of the image of yourself you are shown what is really within. You see inner darkness where loss and gain reside and move beyond to know what truth is. Without feeling there can be no honour to the higher self. The level of fear or light determines the intensity of grief that you experience. When you live truth in life you are stronger in death for its resonance is mightier than that of fear. Out of truth you are taken to the higher ground. Grief helps you to face an inner death. Without this higher perspective you become lost to pain. To forget the higher reason to why grief comes leaves you only to mourn your loss. Grief acts as the reminder to free from the fall. Through personal and external events you are continually living with the potential that sorrow comes again.

GUIDANCE   The more you learn to let go and master the grieving process the lighter you will become. You cannot help but still feel in life for this is to be real but it no longer frightens you to see or know it. Fear and the intensity of grief that you experience are closely related. The more you release the darker shades of yourself that hold you back the easier you will find the integrating of sorrow. This teaching shows us that when we bring in light it will strengthen us in every way. What you are encouraged to do is to persevere in this cause and to not forget.

8.

Release from the heart brings the openness which is essential
to the higher task of dreaming.

In the showing you become connected to higher vibrations.
Release from the heart brings openness which is essential to
the higher task of dreaming. With such an open force you rise
from fear and challenge all that is non-truth within. The highest wish is wholeness. This is the calling that is mightier than
the image of yourself. Where there is not wholeness there
is fear and pain. When you feel wholeness this is the direct
experience of the hallowed expression within. To return to
oneness is the battle for the creative light. This is not a small
journey; only out of perseverance can your true state be reinstated. When open it is the hallowed presence that takes away
what comes with suffering. What becomes fixed in life comes
from the struggle of time where the true self is trying to free
itself from. Through the process of grief is the opportunity for
forgiveness. In this lies freedom with no limits. You no longer
need to be lost in shame and self-punishment for this is the
discord of humanity.

GUIDANCE Joy comes from the freeing in the heart.
Allowing the heart to lead begins with listening to it and releasing the heaviness from it. The heart is the portal to eternal
bliss and through it you reach a place of dreaming that has the
ability to transform everything you know to light. Without the
heart open you cannot reach into the substance of the creative
force that elevates you to the higher dream. This dreaming
starts in you, to sense what is real, to be honest to yourself and

realise that before you can get to your potential, discomfort is part of the journey. Bringing this about is to be active in the responsibility of facing what is heavy in you and to not settle until you find release. People give up because they believe that this is as far as they can go, they can't give more but this reality comes from discord and is far from the truth.

9.

You can use the sensitivity of being to release you from karmic influences that impede your growth.

The task is not to suppress or run away from the intensity of emotion that is now longing to be heard in the heart. Life becomes hard as the heart is made an enemy of. Care is needed for you to remember to find space so that tenderness can exist. In the showing of feelings and to be all that you are without censorship can belief in truth be seen. Truth is derived from the sentiments of the heart that exists beyond the physical. The key to life is in how you create it. In forgetting what lies within you cannot create a life that serves the highest good and so fall to sorrow. In grief is the direct experience of pain where truth follows. You need courage to stay in this mighty place for it is the fire that show's your power. The mind is desperate for peace and believes that peace is found through accumulation and so complicates itself. In this complication it strives for external power and forgets inner truth in order to follow another. Life calls the true self to rise to sustain peace. Out of fear and pain you create the karmic lessons that life brings you in order to push you to learn the higher lessons. You don't have to wait for these lessons. You can use the sensitivity of being to release you from karmic influences that impede your growth. If discord is created in you now, then this will determine the karmic ties that follow you in the next life. Your innate being is searching to expand to oneness and until it does karma will remain to be lived through. The experience of grief in life is the reminder of this separation from the true state of being.

GUIDANCE   All discord derives from a karmic cycle. When you become heightened to the imbalances within and bring them to consciousness you start to break the cycle of karma. Karma is the process of creating equilibrium within you. It only has power over you when you try to ignore pain. When you see what you are experiencing and understand pain this brings transformation. Strengthening the power within is the growing of compassion where the power of love leads and negates the pain of karma.

10.

All that is harmful and all that gives life is the foundation for growth in the next life.

When life is lived in the complete self then you are not lost. You feel the strength of knowing that all is one. That which affects the heart continues with you. All that is harmful and all that gives life is the foundation for growth in the next life. In every fall you experience is the search for surrender to the higher call. It is the strongest sentiments that fill your life that will be carried with you to the next life. All that is heavy in the heart and all that is free is experienced. felt in passing. All that which is heavy in the heart and all that is free is experienced. The higher call is to free yourself and bring about purpose. When you lose self-power in life then the dying process seems unmanageable. The more you become conscious of who you are brings empowerment through the process of death.

GUIDANCE   You do not have to imagine how this may look in your next life as the seeds of what you sow now are being shown to you in your present life. What you do in this moment can be seen as a preparation for the next moment. It's like building blocks if you strengthen and create light in this moment then what will come from this will benefit you. The fruit or sentiments of what you experience govern the growing of what is to come. If you feed and water a plant now you will see the reward of it later and the same happens in life. This is happening at every level of your being, the physical, emotional, mental and energetic. Whichever level you nurture with light will inevitably encourage health and joy in your future self.

11.

Healing the power struggle that lies within is a necessary path for realisation.

Grief remains until such a time that you are released from its illusion. In life there is the existence of fear where you become trapped to time which is hard to bear in the soul. Life asks for you to free from these constraints. All grief experienced is a test to prove yourself to light. Healing the power struggle that lies within is a necessary path for realisation. That which is truth comes from within alone. That which is Holy is the light that carries you always. When the Holy is not made conscious then it becomes hidden and lost to the distortions of life. To live life to the fullest is to know the freedom of being without limitations.

GUIDANCE   The belief that you are lacking in some way comes out of fear. In oneness there is no fear of being more or less than anything else. That this valuing system has nothing to do with higher development is an unshakable truth. You forget to sense the world when you merely compare yourself to it. You see from the heart when you believe through what creates meaning for you. Instead of filling the mind space with the constant worry fuelled from pain have the courage to go within and free yourself into the dream of the heart that knows no power struggle.

12.

Through grief you are reminded of the revelations in life and the path that you choose.

You fight to live life honourably so that you remain whole. That which is the sorrow of grief has become stronger than truth and you become lost in seeking the reasons for your fall. To release from the illusion of such a power struggle is the call to the dream of the self in creating power from within. To gain from external sources traps the self to the place of the physical. In grief is the fight for truth and love. The fight exists because you broke the trust in yourself and now seek to manage. In showing grief is the realisation of what really matters to you. Through grief you are reminded of the revelations in life and the path that you choose.

GUIDANCE   Life finds the perfect ways for us to realise ourselves. In the grieving process it is plain to see that transformations happen at the deepest level. For this reason I hold grief in high esteem. The level of teaching that it offers is vast and this is why so many suffer in it because it is at this point you are tested of how much you have lived the truer part of yourself. To ask for help is a great blessing when you struggle. Others can help to show you the way but it is you that walks the path. To be witnessed brings you powerful insights that remind you of what you have forgotten. Asking for help is not always easy but it may be needed to not pass the opportunity to know yourself further.

13.

In the awakened sense of love there is the knowing of how to live naked, honest and true.

The heart is strong and can withstand any pain if allowed to be all that it is. Many have lost touch with the innocence of their hearts. When the heart leads love becomes the driving power. When courage to follow the longing of the heart is returned then life is guided back towards its higher potential. In the awakened sense of love there is the knowing of how to live naked, honest and true. What shines forth through the creative life force is the eternal flame. This is always flowing and in motion and is the creative process with no beginning or end. Life needs the heart to be fully open and not just designate it for only leisure and play. That which is calling is to come to the true ownership of the higher aspect and to live this. This cannot come from another but comes from the way from within. In your hands alone is the choice to lead a life from a higher place in you and transform reality from suffering to freedom. Freedom is the understanding and awareness of the inner path where there is no more seeking and where all prayers are delivered.

GUIDANCE   This is the higher dream. Joy is created when you are not bound or restricted internally. It is unusual to see but I witness that people fear love and the freedom within them. Why? We function in a simple way, that which is familiar to us makes us feel confident. When we are faced with the unknown even if it is of the highest wish you can resist it. To find love and freedom is to break through barriers. No external experience can give you eternal peace this is your experience alone. Every part of this dream is for empowerment born out of oneness. In you is the knowing presence. To have trust means no matter what unfamiliar terrain you go to you will always know how to carry yourself through it.

Summary of Teachings

1. Sorrow runs deep within not because it is part of the natural state of being but because of the separation from oneness within.

2. The sadness that emanates through grief is the consequence of losing trust and falling to the shame of what you have become.

3. To be honest in how you really feel, to accept fear breeds no further discord inside but frees you into a higher state.

4. The heart feels broken but it is not, in truth it is you opening to the expansion of yourself.

5. When life's processes of struggle and healing present themselves, you are forced to the core of you.

6. We are affected profoundly when we experience an external bereavement and the grief is similar to the internal dying process of the self-image.

7. The level of fear or light determines the intensity of grief that you experience.

8. Release from the heart brings the openness which is essential to the higher task of dreaming.

9. You can use the sensitivity of being to release you from karmic influences that impede your growth.

10. All that is harmful and all that gives life is the foundation for growth in the next life.

11. Healing the power struggle that lies within is a necessary path for realisation.

12. Through grief you are reminded of the revelations in life and the path that you choose.

13. In the awakened sense of love there is the knowing of how to live naked, honest and true.

HEALING YOURSELF GIVES BLESSING FOR OTHERS TO HEAL

UNDERSTAND
forgiveness to yourself releases others from the
burden of suffering

LEARN
how the seed of hope brings relief for others

BELIEVE
you reach light when you walk into the
unknown with courage

1.

To have understanding and meaning in the choices that you
make creates what is real for you.

Modern day freedom is not the same as freedom born out
of higher consciousness. True freedom is not expressed by
the level of choices you make externally or in achieving all
that you desire. To be attached to choices is discord for this
creates a fear of loss. To be free is to not fear because there is
an unshakable knowing of the true essence within. Exploiting
certain aspects of you and deeming others as unacceptable
creates fragmentation. This breeds an internal culture of division, of what you like or dislike in you. When fear is present
and you are unable to understand it then you will continue
to be restricted in some way. When you understand how fear
manifests and why it has come then you move past it and
heal the wound that it is masking. Turning outwards you give
power away. You seek to gain to fill the void you feel internally. To have understanding and meaning in the choices that
you make creates what is real for you.

GUIDANCE   When you make a choice by being guiding
from what feels real then this has the ability to change the
quality of life. Each time you lead from the heart force you
create an invincible power of will that can drive your vision
forward. This is how you create reality by making choices from
an empowered place. When you choose out of trying to please
others or adapt what feels meaningful for you, to fit in you
become a diluted version of yourself. Fill the substance of your
life with the abundant vital energy that comes when you free
who you are and not limit it.

2.

To light the way you must will truth.

With every release in healing you grow stronger. Untethering the self from fear and the wounds that lie within untethers you to holding on to the past, present or future. The wound is karmic meaning you need to learn something from it in order to grow. Until you transform this wound through direct experience then you stay tied to a past experience. By fearing past experiences you attach to the future to find relief. Pain and suffering create this dynamic where time controls you. You are not here only to free from karma, for this is a small part of your higher potential. This is the stepping stone to learning how to master you. You live karma because through this you learn higher life lessons. Because of treason within karma exists. To light the way you must will truth. The purpose of karma is to free from the illusion of that which ties you down and to believe again in truth. Trust is regained through the exploration of you. The growing of trust within helps you realise hope for the higher dream that lies beyond all discord.

GUIDANCE   To understand your will is to have clarity. In a time of information overload where you are asked to follow without the presence of mind you are used to being a bystander. You lose clarity when you become absent. Every time you follow without inner awareness you weaken your will power. To strengthen the will is to stop and to consciously know why you are choosing this path. Clarity comes to you when you see the motivation behind your intentions. Ask why are you doing this? What is it that motivates you in this moment? Start with the bigger processes of your life and explore what this means to you. You know when your truth is present if the answer you give is helping to strengthen light. Each time you choose consciously to do that which lifts you, you grow power of will.

3.

Your being naturally continues to reach towards oneness and search for its wholeness for this is what it knows.

The calling of the heart will show you back to wholeness. By mastering the challenge that pain brings, you move past struggle. What has been hardship leads you to stray from the true self, to lose faith within and turn outwards to follow others. Your being naturally continues to reach towards oneness and search for its wholeness for this is what it knows. To lose trust has made you turn your back on feeling. For long enough you moved with caution to allowing feelings to lead. When courage grows and the leap into the darkness is taken then finding light can be faced with confidence.

GUIDANCE   Regardless if these teachings touch you or not life will always bring you what you need. The creative expression is always unfolding in exactly the way it knows how whether you are conscious of it or not. In the higher wisdom of what is carried through all of us can the answers to life be understood. The evolutionary path has asked us to know suffering to know light. These higher truths seek to lift the veil to the nature of living without suffering. What you believe matters and this guides you. To open is to bring that which lies in your subconscious to consciousness, for this division was created through the separation of the oneness state.

4.

For many the journey to oneness can be filled with pain as they resist seeing their frailties.

You are responsible for all that you create in life. What you do that is life giving and loving does not tie you for it is pure and flowing in energy. All that creates discord corrupts the flow of being and so must be undone through you to flow freely again. When our energy does not flow health and well-being is profoundly affected. This is creations way of healing you, this is how karma works. All that is karmic and tethers the soul to the past is here to seek resolve and harmony. These wounds become our teachers. For many the journey to oneness can be filled with pain as they resist seeing their frailties. This path has been blinded by endless escapes and past times. Through this divine plan we are given the exact circumstances to come to truth of being and light. What was once precious from within has become dulled, devalued and purposeless. What you do in life becomes empowered when you are able to create from meaning within you. To do this you must know the self and understand the true essence of what is happening inside of you.

GUIDANCE   People come to healing to find the support to have courage to see their self. To witness pain is resisted because for so long you have sought answers outside of you.

This has been a habit and so turning inwards is like swimming against a strong tide, the effort needed is more than you realise. I see how people give their self a hard time, turning against their self for feeling as lost as they do. To be lost is not a failure it is a part of the journey to light. It is when you walk into the darkness of yourself and walk to the edge of what you know that you regain truth. Getting side tracked in making yourself feel worse cannot help you. Instead you create yet another distraction from the real task which is to be with fear and come to know it.

5.

In living you have choice of how you become, what you pursue and what leads you.

There are endless ways of trying to protect yourself from the pain in the heart. Release in the heart is the opening to the nature of the true self. With a free heart the prayer to grow light is clear. Through the sentiments in the heart can reality be transformed for the highest good. On earth are the perfect conditions to live into the light self. In living you have choice of how you become, what you pursue and what leads you. The creative life force is not your enemy. It does not wish to disempower you as this belief comes from discord. In the harshness of life many are overwhelmed and now fear what is in the heart.

GUIDANCE   To be the leader of yourself is to trust in your abilities to lead. Do you inspire yourself? Answering this gives you a good idea of the connection you have to the essence of you. Learning to love that which comes from yourself is not some romantic ideal but hard work. The journey to the heart holds many twists and turns that have already scared you and made you feel powerless. To bring back trust asks of you to listen to what you feel when you are vulnerable and when you feel strong. Showing is to reveal what you come with because by doing this you base life on the strong foundation of truth.

6.

When you heal yourself you release others from the toxicity of the wound in you and give blessing for them to heal.

The attachment to achieving outside the self continues to tether and stunt personal growth. When the heart does not feed the soul you fall into a place of pain. In the seeds of your convictions is the path of freeing from pain. Freedom is found from within. This opens the path to the light. Understanding pain in yourself brings empathy for others. From healing you know the cause of your pain. This has a profound effect on all those concerned too. When you heal yourself you release others from the toxicity of the wound in you and give blessing for them to heal also. Forgiving what you carry means another can be forgiven too. When you have humility then there is the potential to connect to another's pain.

GUIDANCE   Your thoughts and feelings of disharmony resonate from the experience of difficult past relationships, and may even affect the way you relate to people today. Holding on to pain can continues to create unease in how you relate to others. In healing, the release of tensions means that you have the opportunity to forgive as you take responsibility of feelings and thoughts. Discord creates a feeling of unease in the whole of your being and for a long time you have not walked in your truth. We are fragile and in truth are as sensitive as young children. Many have suppressed this natural state of love and acceptance for in their pain they have turned away from their self. Forgiveness must start in you and then when you are free you free all those concerned. When you still find you cannot forgive others then you have more to heal within.

7.

When you are vulnerable you are closest to light.

When you feel despair you lose hope. Hope comes when you find meaning in pain. Through seeing, you free from the grip of fear, for without this you cannot realise the innate power in you. Love is when the higher self is open and here lies hope. What is real is what moves you through suffering. When there is love then the Holy within creation can live to open its self. When you are vulnerable you are closest to light. You have the courage to break through the borders of yourself and see the realness in you. To show is to deliver the shower of light and to walk the Holy way. When you go slowly you listen to the inner self for this is what is yearning to be balanced. This is prayer. When you are able to listen to what is true for you then this delivers light.

GUIDANCE   To be in the light aspect of you draws light to you, this is the law of attraction. Your heightened sensitivity allows you to decipher what is meaningful to you in a truer way. The more in tune to the authentic self the more you have the ability to create the world you want to live in. The state of vulnerability is showing you the way. The next time you feel agitated or anxious see if you can pause and not try to escape it. Notice if you can track when you started to feel it and the reason that may have triggered this. Not knowing why you suddenly feel anxiety makes you feel disorientated. Anxiety is a helpful warning sign that knows when something does not feel right for you. The hurdle for many is to accept this sensitivity and follow what it is trying to show them.

8.

Hope is infectious for very few can carry this light in them.

To live without borders opens the door for others too. To offer yourself in the healing process carries forward the hope into life. Hope is infectious for very few can carry this light in them. What you do affects everything and everyone. Being in light is the gift of heaven on earth. When you feel what you are present and strong you can't help but release this to all around you. The potential to move towards oneness derives from here. Fears cannot play a prominent role if you strengthen through healing. If you do not forget this then you will come to freedom. Living with sensitivity requires you to have courage, for this sensitivity must be expressed to grow. Those who feel they struggle and lock away their sensitivity must realise that this is where power lies.

GUIDANCE   You have the inner knowing to change life to serve light, you are able to find solutions at every crossroad, you do not fear pain but embrace its call to you, you listen to all you are and embody truth in peace and love. This positive affirmation that you can remind yourself of is hope. To have hope within is a powerful force. Hope lies in you each time you triumph in the journey to inner knowing. When you witness that which is truth you feel the essence of which you are and what makes you. To have self-belief brings about hope.

9.

From a divided inner reality feelings become separate from thought and consciousness separate from the sub-conscious.

Being separated from the true self begins the search to wholeness. In lifetimes you come to know the distortions that are created from this separate reality. The path to empowerment is the higher teaching. The disconnection forces you to relate to others with division between you and them. You consider life from your needs only and move away from life being a shared experience. From a divided inner reality feelings become separate from thought and consciousness separate from the sub-conscious. When you make an enemy of feeling terror is created and so you fill life with escapes and avoidance. The intention of why you do something needs to be clear, for vulnerability and doubt surface quickly. To reinstate self-belief and be free from restrictions is why you face the shadow self. In every fear faced there is the potential to meet with truth. Every inner battle won brings forth a release of higher teachings for soul growth. This is permanent and sustaining. Belief that is created from truth creates that which is purposeful in life. This creates meaning and is able to serve the greater good. Through the illumination of you comes self-belief.

GUIDANCE   Oneness exists with no division, with no borders that hold parts of you apart. A divided reality tries to withhold a sense of protection, to limit what we have in order to continue to preserve the self. This exists because of fear within. Without fear you accept all that is within and outside yourself. In acceptance there is no formula to life. These teachings urge you to listen to what's real in you but this experience is not shut off from the world. To feel the sensitivity within means you are able to feel the sensitivity in another. There are no hard and fast rules to living life. You must feel life and make the choice that is the truest to you based on all the information presented to you from what is inside of you and outside. Life is a co-creation and you are not separate from the world.

10.

Cultivating life from the heart is to be in direct connection to the eternal self so that the divine can express its blessing.

To experience the infinite parts of you, you must move through the heart force. By its very nature the heart essence has no limits, knows no boundaries and experiences life as an expansion of itself. It is the portal for the divine aspect of self to express itself from. This can create a higher state of living which is true happiness and not happiness derived from self-gaining. When the heart is free to express itself then perfect living follows. Cultivating life from the heart is to be in direct connection to the eternal self so that the divine can express its blessing. Know that this reality is not given to only the privileged few but is attainable for all.

GUIDANCE   When new to healing many people fear feeling too much. You may feel this when you experience life mainly through thought and you may question life a lot. This has kept you safe from having to feel too much. In such cases the healing process can seem daunting for it asks you to move from the head into the heart. Undoing a potential lifetime of not connecting within is a slow process. It may come with discomfort and feeling directionless but it requires of you perseverance to not lose hope and to surround yourself with those who support your empowerment.

11.

What is real and what is an illusion can be confusing.

What is real and what is an illusion can be confusing. By turning inwards self-belief and the path to the higher fire can be realised. To find what is calling you is to breathe life into truth and live it. Hope comes when you realise how to show yourself without limits. To feel into what lies within, all pain, disharmony or joy opens you to light. This path illuminates the way to the true self and to freedom from suffering. When there is freedom in the heart then love is let in. When the heart is allowed to be all that it is then there is love. In the fracture of the self you have opportunity to see your reflection and move out of the separateness of being to return to wholeness.

GUIDANCE   What is real comes with light, health, truth and love. To refine yourself in any way helps facilitate this inner process. For example all physical practices that detoxify, cleanse and release the body from toxins will encourage the process at all levels of being. Your sensitivity is enhanced the more you lighten any part of you no matter whether you work on the physical, emotional, mental or spiritual plane. Know that any act that you do that helps to lighten you is clearing the way for the well-being of your future self. Each part of you can enhance the higher sensitivity of being. The act of knowing comes from awareness, refine yourself at any level and you accelerate your growth.

12.

When grief comes it is creations way to lift you from the monotony of how life has become and realign you to what feels real to you.

Life is given to know love, through the heart of being. The choice is in your hands to harness what lies in you. Without conscious thought and acts intending to find truth you drift and become lost to outside distraction. When grief comes it is creations way to lift you from the monotony of how life has become and realign you to what feels real to you. When you experience sorrow you are reminded to not forget this higher call. To live what feels real comes out of the pureness of the heart. The potential of life is amazing, for you naturally will seek to pull your way through. Life creates processes for you to search for the inner fire and to live light.

GUIDANCE   The intensity of grief has the ability to shift reality effectively out of everyday seeing. When you experience grief you become numb to the outside world and are forced to go within. When your higher intelligence calls you have to face pain in the heart as it draws your attention away from the external reality. This process is a blessing for us to heal. To be in grief is the closest many go in the potential of experiencing their true self. To be familiar to this process helps you to navigate your way through. Healing will come to you one way or another for this is life. To live in harmony the heart will continue to seek balance.

13.

When faith is installed in you others can wish to know it too.

The essence of you is incorrupt and unlimited. In the realisation of oneness lies no struggle or need for control. Self-belief is replaced by indifference and powerlessness. When truth emanates into the world then an invincible faith is created for this is what is gained inside of you. When realised it is imagined by others too. Through the self is a gateway opened for others to see their potential. Through the power of prayer and in the calling of the higher self is light created for others too. In healing the seeds of hope for others are planted. It is not that others need to follow blindly. It is a consciousness that emanates through the true self that they witness. In turn can they remember their own light. When faith is installed in you others can wish to know it too.

GUIDANCE   Our energy effects everything around us, light uplifts and pain weighs us down. Light comes through the unlimited self and pain from discord. Expressing truth does not seek validation from another but to move with an open heart that has the potential to create miracles around you. For empowerment you must know your truth alone. To see each other as victims cannot help but merely conditions further discord. Belief within you helps to restore the belief in the potential of another. You do not need to rescue or fear another's path. Just like you they are given the exact circumstances that they need to grow their light. You can be helped to come to the edge of your fear but it must be your choice to step into the unknown. Sometimes this is as far as you can go, to force is unnecessary as you have to do this when you are ready too. It may be years before you can or in extreme cases lifetimes, but in the true processes of life there lies no time. Each step is not wasted but builds a life giving memory of courage on the path to your empowerment.

That which has been will be again.

Summary of Teachings

1. To have understanding and meaning in the choices that you make creates what is real for you.

2. To light the way you must will truth.

3. Your being naturally continues to reach towards oneness and search for its wholeness for this is what it knows.

4. For many the journey to oneness can be filled with pain as they resist seeing their frailties.

5. In living you have choice of how you become, what you pursue and what leads you.

6. When you heal yourself you release others from the toxicity of the wound in you and give blessing for them to heal.

7. When you are vulnerable you are closest to light.

8. Hope is infectious for very few can carry this light in them.

9. From a divided inner reality feelings become separate from thought and consciousness separate from the sub-conscious.

10. Cultivating life from the heart is to be in direct connection to the eternal self so that the divine can express its blessing.

11. What is real and what is an illusion can be confusing.

12. When grief comes it is creations way to lift you from the monotony of how life has become and realign you to what feels real to you.

13. When faith is installed in you others can wish to know it too.

III

YOUR CHOICE

LET GO OF CONTROL

UNDERSTAND
what you want and give attention to creates reality

LEARN
how feeling powerless makes you want to control
another

BELIEVE
through the knowing of separation do you come
to union

1.

Internal imbalance is not sustainable as hardship and further discord follows.

In life has come a passion to care for nothing. To seek for harmony becomes lost to indifference. The creative force that lives within cannot be tamed or controlled for discord is formed. When the life force is oppressed then the need to control is born from it. From this disconnect you fear the loss of control and so you will demand control in other parts of life. You become subject to worry, anxieties and suffering. Internal imbalance is not sustainable as hardship and further discord follows. The purpose of returning to life on earth is to correct this imbalance and to heal inner wounds that have rendered the heart powerless. Through karma you learn to do this. With direct experience of what you feel can you be untethered from karmic ties.

GUIDANCE   In the nature of the soul there lies this constant struggle, what you experience internally and what you need externally. This dynamic pushes and pulls you in a fight against yourself. Out of fear or habit you do not meet this unease but give attention to what feels more important outside of you. To turn your gaze inwards addresses this tension. Beginning to look inside is the task; the direction of your energy is conditioned to move outwards to the external reality. What is crucial to this teaching is that you create higher meaning in life through the internal experience. There is no division. To ignore internal imbalance brings about further discord where you feel out of touch.

2.

Life can become rigid and forced to fit into the constructs of the mind.

Life becomes rigid and forced to fit into the constructs of the mind. These hard structures govern and control experience and so create insensitivity. In the need to control, life becomes dulled for the fear of uncertainty penetrates. To fixate comes from a restricted place attached to time and space. You cannot live the mystery of life from this reality for freedom cannot be achieved this way. That which lies beyond all pain takes you to the unlimited self. To master living free you must face fear. To let go of control is to allow feeling to be and face the unknown. To live a higher reality is to come home, to realign to truth and to weave with the pattern of life and not against it.

GUIDANCE   How you create life matters. When you want to know how things will unfold this limits your experience of life. For example, you have a thought that you need to sort out a disagreement with someone. When you allow thought to lead, you imagine the best outcome for you. You aim for this expectation and try to achieve this goal. When you come to the person you stay focused on what you want to happen. What actually happens is the person wants something else and this makes you feel stuck. To move from thought alone fixates if you attach to certain imagined outcomes. By letting go of control you welcome the element of the unknown and you can listen freely without the need to fix the outcome. To trust in life you must have heart connection.

3.

*When you feel a void within you seek fulfilment from outside
and so will try to dominate life.*

It happens so quickly, to want, to accumulate and acquire that you become blind to this subtle oppressor. To demand externally is to be separated from the true state within. In this wanting you live with expectations but the greater the expectation the higher we have to fall. To expect is the distorted expression of control. When you feel a void within you seek fulfilment from outside and try to dominate life. Domination is created from a place of discord and so forces demands on life. You must seriously question this sense of lack in you to be able to conquer the need to control. In the original state you know yourself complete. In being disengaged from the true self you experience the feeling of separation within and to the world. This feeling causes great difficulties and forces you to function out of an individualistic nature. The cultivation of individualism for the purpose of gain in the world creates all manner of corruption and fear. Fulfilment cannot come from a place of disconnection from the true self for it breeds self-preservation. To live free from corruption and inhibition is to know no boundaries within.

GUIDANCE   Disconnection makes you feel like you are empty inside, nervous because the foundation of you is not strong. What is the void you seek to escape? That which feels empty in you is life's mystery that holds within it a new script as it is the unfolding of higher processes that are not predetermined or pre-planned. To not imagine this scares you and to stay in the known traps you to the fear of losing control. When you want to force an outcome you dominate. Release comes when you heal the fear you have of letting go. This teaching comes when you face fear and learn to strengthen the foundation within you.

4.

Pleasure experienced through the physical outer realm is but transitory for it is conditional and relies on external factors for it to exist.

The innate knowing that light is calling you back brings grief, for it is the consequence of the separation from the oneness state. This loss creates a power struggle and it becomes a necessity to dominate life. Out of the wounded heart and fear, suffering is created. Pleasure experienced through the physical outer realm is but transitory for it is conditional and relies on external factors for it to exist. Searching for bliss through the physical world alone has lost the higher path. Attaching to the outer world breeds the sentiments of resistance to letting go, for to hold on you fear that eventually you will have to let go. Out of attachment and control the toxic energies of anger, hate, envy and resentment are seeded. To free physical, emotional and mental inhibitions within you turn inwards.

GUIDANCE   Life conditions you to chase your dream and to fulfil this dream outside of you. The wave of this movement must change if we are to change our reality to the higher light. This teaching shows that everlasting peace comes from a source inside of you. The ever changing processes externally cannot sustain you. We have to avoid trying to imagine what the essence of joy feels like for it cannot come from an attached place. This experience comes in the direct connection to the forces at play within you and that has no conditions. To dream and follow your wish is healthy but holding on too tightly cannot help you.

5.

Remaining captive to constraints within cannot reveal to you what is real in the physical world.

Life on earth is given to develop the highest aspect of you. What lies beyond the struggle of light and dark is truth of the Holy creation. To want to claim, own and control is the biggest downfall. This power struggle tricks you into a game. Without letting go of control you stay blind to the higher goal. Courage now is needed to explore the self carefully and to master what is real. Remaining captive to constraints cannot reveal to you what is true in the physical world. In life is the opportunity to embrace and learn about the nature of you, and create out of the greater potential in the physical world. When lived, this ultimate truth seeks not to control for it is free unto itself. In this realisation an eternal gateway is opened and you are released from limitation.

GUIDANCE   To create a world that feels true to you is to know freedom within. All borders place limits to what you feel is safe and what you do not. You will only see what you want to see in the outside world and this is governed through a wish to stay safe. Feeling unsafe internally will colour how you feel externally. When you remain distant to feeling what is real for you this shows that your sensitivity is struggling to be aware of what is real outside of you. When free to roam internally governs how free you are externally. Bringing light within will carve a truer path for you without.

6.

The creative force moves freely through the spheres of love in the heart and this alchemy is the powerful and sustaining force.

To realise the inner realm you must give it attention. When impulses are driven with clear intention from what is real then you create with life giving energy. The creative force moves freely through the spheres of love in the heart and this alchemy is the powerful and sustaining force. This journey challenges you to trust, for you are asked to walk into the inner depths. Through liberating the soul from corruption can you open and live the promise of the Holy. You can see how the world resonates with a tender nature. Cleansing the soul from the dullness of life raises your vibration. Karmic discord must be untethered for you to reinstate your wholeness. Making this process conscious is how you learn to be the creator of reality. With direct seeing the process of healing can bring grace. It is the sentiments of this expression that bring you to the knowing of who you are. Life does not exist for outcomes or for an ending. All that exists has no need for validation or confirmation. When life is explored through the higher essence of the self then you will transform reality.

GUIDANCE   All that sustains you unconditionally comes from within. That which lives through the sensitivity of being is the knowing of this creative life force that moves through the whole of life. Its force is all powerful and reminds you of what you are. It is the sacred origins of home where your true essence is felt and where all higher opening is moving to be aligned with. It is the substance that connects life. This is not the love that is depicted in main stream culture but is the element that connects you to the vital force. It is the channel of which you move through to reach the higher potential. To come to this you must know freedom in the heart and let go of the attachments that restrict you.

7.

After death your sentiments are what propel you towards the conditions of the next life.

To realise conscious living in this life time is the gift of life. The chance to learn and experience about you is here, right now. All the sentiments absorbed into you, all that you feel the strongest about and all that you desire creates you. After death the sentiments are what propel you towards the conditions of the next life. The magnificence of the earth offers the most perfect environment as the vehicle for transcendence. In the processes of life is the opportunity to develop and discover your true nature and return to oneness. In the human form you are given a powerful force, the freedom of will. In each moment of life there is the choice to respond in one way or another, to seek one thing over another. That which you give attention to effects the reality you create and that which you are becoming. If you only desire to gain outside of you and become lost then the reality of accumulation and physical gratification is what you breed into life. This reality cannot free you from suffering but rather feeds it. You transform the quality of life through self-belief and from that which is meaningful to you. To pay attention to the inner world is to be aware of what you feel, think and believe in. All that has true value in life is found inside of you.

GUIDANCE   We are exploring the eternal essence of you and the influence you have on shaping reality. This truth reveals that what you feel, think and believe brings about a profound impact on what you are becoming. You are a ball of energy that has the ability to steer itself. The shape, texture, weight and look of you are in your hands. What you do now is the investment in the future self. Feelings and thoughts are you; they are energy that creates the movement of you. Every vibration that emanates from you has the ability to move you in one direction or another, to come to certain people and situations over others. To create light and live what is real in you forms the solid foundations for your future.

8.

*Power struggles come from the wish to own and you become
lost to this purpose.*

Creating without attachment releases you from the past and the future. Through the sentiments of the heart in present time, can the response to life's call be created sensitively. The colours and vibrations of life can be distinguished and the essence of you seen. By discerning the energies through feeling can life be intuited and you can be sure that this comes from what is life giving. To function out of the discord of the self you seek to gain for the self. You become lost in trade and ownership and seek to manipulate life for it. Power struggles come from the wish to own and you become lost to this purpose. Corruption is created in the name of ownership. This is a widely accepted construct based on fear of human survival. It has been forgotten that which sustains you cannot come from the physical realm. In the modern world this higher wisdom is ignored and makes life hard and insensitive. Being caught in this reality you must tread carefully to move away from it.

GUIDANCE   It seems that what is yours or mine, matters in the world. How you become affected by ownership is an interesting process to reveal. Imagine the moment before you acquire something, you have always been used to yourself without this in your life. Now let us sense the inner change that happens when you own. You can feel happy, elated, inspired or disappointed whatever you feel now becomes a part of you. In owning you become attached to it because you are attached to the way it makes you feel. For example it is easy to give away something that is not fulfilling you in some way, for you don't want to encourage that feeling. The image of yourself becomes tied to ownership and you attach to this image of you. External gain does not sustain you but it is for the vanity of your self-image.

9.

To impose values does not come from light but from that which
disempowers you.

Instead of growing the innate sensitivity within there is
the active promotion of life being lived through commodity.
What really matters cannot be solved this way. You are unable
to achieve the sovereignty of being through the promotion of
ownership and the distribution of it. This happens through
the expression of truth through the absolute knowing that
all power is equal for all. To impose values does not come
from light but from that which disempowers you. The core of
letting go of control is to free from the constructs of ownership. You will believe that power comes through what you
own. The collective experience is being propelled to turn
outwards to meet this criteria and the inner reality becomes
unimportant for it does not promote this cause. Life is based
on accumulation, achievements and the fixation of outcomes
and returns. Living this has left an empty void within where
true meaning becomes absent.

GUIDANCE   What is better or worse for you must be judged
by you. When we judge and compare each other we do so
from the collective belief of what has value and what doesn't.
Judging another spreads the pain of comparing. This higher
truth comes from the principle that there exists no hierarchy,
that value is only constructed to suit our ends. What arrives
with an aggressive force is not truth but a distortion of it, for
the love of light does not know this place of fear. Living into
light helps you see that all is equal. Who is better or worse,

higher or lower, more advanced means nothing unless you are invested in its value system. Such a system does not come from light. Truth lies beyond this and cannot be disempowered by the opinions of others. Know your truth and you will have an unshakable power of will.

10.

Knowing that in truth you own nothing helps you turn within to see your truth and breaks the illusion of an outer power leading you.

To invest in an external power diminishes the higher potential of evolution. To live for this purpose is not life giving and must eventually seek to destroy itself. Life is asking to awaken to its true self. For new life the old ways must cease to be and this starts with inner knowing. Being the master of destiny can be carefully realised and freedom from struggle will occur. The impact of attachment and ownership has profound effect on you psychologically. The fear of losing what you have, continually seeks your attention. These sentiments have bred the need for self-preservation on a collective scale for you believe ownership creates security. In this fight, the principle truth is that nothing is yours. Only greed and the constant search for self-assurance are created by fear of loss. Knowing that in truth you own nothing helps you turn within breaks the illusion of an outer power leading you.

GUIDANCE   Bolstering the image of yourself does not serve you but diminishes power. You are not weak but you are easily led. This is a great challenge, for to stand out from the crowd forces you to face the fear of loneliness. Cutting the tie to this reality can push you to feeling lost. Through all healing processes this place is essential to reach. It is not because you will remain there or fall into the depths of despair but for you to know you have nothing and you must face it inside of you. To realise this is freedom. In this void fear comes to prepare you to see what is real for you. You remain following that outside of you if you try to escape this space inside of you. When you reach the place where you are empty and alone and have courage to not runaway you face fear and learn what lives beyond it.

11.

The experience that aggression is commonly used to acquire power leads you to believe that you need force to have empowerment.

The experience that aggression is commonly used to acquire power leads you to believe that you need force to have empowerment. By holding on, to fight for the right to own you believe this attains power. Force realises pain. To move past fear you must see that nothing is actually lost, for it was never owned in the first place. This is a manmade construct that has been developed out of the distortion within and creates the instability that mankind exists from. The unshakable knowledge that you are part of everything and own nothing is a higher truth. Raising the vibrational state helps you lead a life that opens you to further possibilities. To move away from self-gaining principles is to discern what is true and what is not. Security is sustainable when it lives out of the oneness of being, that is complete and life giving in nature. In fear is the reality of isolation, separation and loneliness. By losing the connection to the higher aspects of being a hardship in life is created. In facing this transitory hardship you move towards the liberated self.

GUIDANCE   To equate love with empowerment is not the most widely interpreted version. Light is empowerment and this is through the awakening of the higher self within the physical reality. This remains divided until there is a safe space for you to show a higher sensitivity. The calling is to integrate this higher sensitivity into the whole of your life and not just when a sacred space is created. Love knows no boundaries and this potential is the evolutionary path. Becoming is opening yourself and releasing that which makes you hide or feel heavy. You cannot do this in a ruthless way for this comes from discord. Happiness is intrinsic to being and not something you need to acquire; this has always been there behind the many layers that mask the true essence of you.

12.

Directly seeing that the true being knows no harm can liberate you from the illusion of suffering.

Liberation of the soul comes from the knowledge in the depths of being. Self-preservation comes when there is movement out of fear. In light there is no need to preserve yourself for there is already the invincible knowledge of sovereignty. Directly seeing that the true being knows no harm can liberate you from the illusion of suffering. To come to this freedom is the greatest wish, the one true purpose in life and the highest hope. There is no need then to prove, to follow another or search, there is just knowing.

GUIDANCE   When you hold a lot of pain out of protection, you can feel anger, and in its worse form hate. Life becomes very complicated when the discord within is strong. Love is simple; truth is strong but not aggressive. Love and reason are the greatest healers for the hardest of pains. To punish, judge or criticise only fuels further pain. To be empowered is to wish all to move towards empowerment. Light is abundantly more powerful than pain and discord. Light can guide you through anything but to know it you must walk through the darkness and when this is too strong you can ask for guidance.

13.

To open the borders within, you must see that all that is created in you is your responsibility.

If life is built within borders then seeking control follows. You think defending what you believe keeps you safe. This has caused all manner of distraction from the true self. Self-discovery allows for the understanding of the inner realm. To do this there needs to be movement without restriction. Placing trust in yourself comes through the innate knowledge of a higher intelligence that brings you to the right place.

To open the borders within, you must see that all that is created in you is your responsibility. The ability to enlighten the self comes from you and cannot be given to you from another. To this end no one is created differently. All have the potential to achieve oneness. It is not merely for the gifted or the elite, it is achievable by all and that potential waits for you if you wish it.

GUIDANCE   Inner trust is achieved when you take responsibility of what you have created. To open or close your inner world is always a choice, what you do is in your hands. As sentient beings we affect each other but cannot walk a path of truth for another. Understanding and accepting how you came to be who you are is the first step to changing your future. Healing is not about reaching a crises and then being forced to see pain. We can live with healing as an integrated part of daily life. To change the development of evolution towards light we must seek ways to live in harmony with the showing of what we carry. Encouraging and accepting this in each other makes this change smoother and possible.

Summary of Teachings

1. Internal imbalance is not sustainable as hardship and further discord follows.

2. Life can become rigid and forced to fit into the constructs of the mind.

3. When you feel a void within you seek fulfilment from outside and so will try to dominate life.

4. Pleasure experienced through the physical outer realm is but transitory for it is conditional and relies on external factors for it to exist.

5. Remaining captive to constraints within cannot reveal to you what is real in the physical world.

6. The creative force moves freely through the spheres of love in the heart and this alchemy is the powerful and sustaining force.

7. After death your sentiments are what propel you towards the conditions of the next life.

8. Power struggles come from the wish to own and you become lost to this purpose.

9. To impose values does not come from light but from that which disempowers you.

10. Knowing that in truth you own nothing helps you turn within to see your truth and breaks the illusion of an outer power leading you.

11. The experience that aggression is commonly used to acquire power leads you to believe that you need force to have empowerment.

12. Directly seeing that the true being knows no harm can liberate you from the illusion of suffering.

13. To open the borders within, you must see that all that is created in you is your responsibility.

PROTECTING YOURSELF PREVENTS LOVE FROM COMING IN

UNDERSTAND
that protecting yourself divides and limits
expression

LEARN
how your true nature can be replaced by
a false self to fit in

BELIEVE
it is through opening the heart that the
capacity to receive love grows

1.

When you rely solely on truth, then you become strengthened to live into the tenderness of the heart, where love is accessed through the power of the creative force.

In the surrendering to what lies within, you open to love. When you close the heart from pain and suffering then you turn outwards to find a replacement love. Surrendering is when you choose to open to what is truth in you without hiding, escaping or justification. You feel this is a sacrifice. To surrender is likened to giving in and losing the battle, but you can never truly win the external battle. When you rely solely on truth, you become strengthened to live into the tenderness of the heart, where love is accessed through the power of the creative force. The creative life force and love become one when the heart lives free. When you heal this allows for the heart to open further where there lays the potential for awakening to be accelerated. Consciously choosing to open through suffering is what brings self-belief. What is important is the wish to choose to be yourself and surrender to all you are. The illusion of fighting an external battle has been the fall from the higher self. Belief in the self is created out of the wish for it and it awakens the living power within. Remembering this is key to unfolding light.

GUIDANCE   The yearning for love mirrors the higher call to return to the truest essence of you. The power of love is unmistakable for it has the ability to face all odds. Reason cannot slow it down or destroy it for when it is lived you are supported with a mighty force. You search for love outside yourself to fill the void within. Love needs nothing but to express its joy and light. The greatest experience of love lies within and this must be wished for to become manifest. When we believe that love comes with external attachment and conditions this is discord. You struggle to follow what is true to you because of the fear that you will not be loved by others. Each time you turn inwards you face yourself, for many this scares them. Truth bears all and this can make you feel exposed and vulnerable. Know that discomfort is part of the journey to opening and you must take care within it.

2.

In protecting yourself, you separate from being connected to another and create a divide that fuels judgement and criticism.

To create from inner fire there must be the sense of freedom within. You cannot show all that you are if you protect yourself from the fear of pain. What lies behind pain is truth. The hardness in life makes you feel forced to have protection. You place a shield around the heart to stop you feeling too much within this harsh reality. You become vigilant to that which helps you and that which hurts. In protecting yourself, you separate from being connected to another and create a divide that fuels judgement and criticism. The effect of protecting yourself restricts the growth of love. To lose trust within creates these borders.

GUIDANCE   To live this way dramatically changes the quality of life. The wall you place around you creates distance instantly. You can be guarded and unsure as the world will seem an unsafe place to live in. This in turn is what the world sees in you. When you live in a guarded way then life will bring to you those paths that emanate at the same frequency. You gravitate to others who are forced to judge from their insecurities also. Life then becomes full of restrictions and criticism which does not allow the soul to breathe. You become trapped in external beliefs which take you even further from inner knowing. To take down these walls you turn inwards to find inner strength. You have the ability to change this way of being by releasing the wounds of the heart.

3.

You invoke protection to shield yourself from pain.

You believe in a false safety, for that which you really fear is within you. You invoke protection to shield yourself from pain. Protection exists out of fear and has come from the price of the fall. Inner fire is the force of innate strength flowing freely being all that it needs to be. In fear and discord that comes out of the corruption you can choose to face pain and free your fire. Without the foundation of truth you battle to live into the higher potential. We drift in the fall for self-belief is weak. When you look to find hope inside of you then it will come. To feel into what you came for is to find your way back to the Holy. In the opening to that which is real, you find hope.

GUIDANCE   You believe that you must be guarded because you feel others can harm you. The nature of the soul invokes protection, not for the reason that it stops others harming, but because of the pain that exists within us. When there exists no fear within then you will have nothing to fear outside of you. In fact you are guarding yourself from yourself. This is the internal trap that we exist with. Learning to trust comes each time you face fear and build an alliance back to the self. The extent to which you are guarded mirrors how much you fear the pain in you.

4.

Without feeling there is no true connection.

The true self is created from a supersensitive reality which is aligned to an unlimited creative force. The structure of modern life moves away from this original source. Without this sensitivity you make an enemy of feeling and replace it with the distorted tyranny that comes out of the mind. Without feeling there is no true connection. You come to the essence of the heart self when you feel and this is what informs thoughts. Without the balance of the heart and mind you are forced to live from thought impulses and function in isolation imposing specific outcomes on life. This is the experience of control. To control you attach to these outcomes.

GUIDANCE   What we are differentiating here is the quality of the life force when you create out of the mind alone and not with feeling. The mind energy is calculative, distant and hard. When you come into the heart force this flow is expansive, open and light and is able to meet the world around it. Emotion and thought are energy but with different qualities and purpose. The power of belief comes from the mind but if your belief originates through thought alone as can happen when you follow another you become empty of the heart force. When power of belief comes from the heart informing your belief then you create from a true and higher place. Without feeling you lose the connection to yourself and the outer world.

5.

Expecting comes from forcing, control and is aggressive by nature.

Empowerment is the reflection of freedom that you live inside and not externally. This means freedom from pain, suffering, corruption, division, and carelessness, all that is not true in the divine self. From a place of discord you start to have expectations of what you should be and try to force truth. Expecting comes from forcing, control and is aggressive by nature. To expect is desire from a place of fear that is struggling with not knowing. Without self-belief you cannot be realised. The true self has to be directly experienced for this is real. Self-realisation is waking to the higher self of being; this cannot be pre-meditated or given to you by another but is yours to see directly. Through the agitation of seeking that which you demand can prevent light from being.

GUIDANCE   This higher truth may challenge you for to expect is commonplace. But its origin comes from a place of discord and not from the true state of being. This sentiment brings the subtle force of aggression because you want it so much you become bound to it until it's achieved. In the healing process a great challenge is to let go of the attachment of what you were expecting or what you feel you should have had. The pain of loss runs deep through us. Much time can be spent on helping people to let go. To let go is to realise that truth cannot lie in your expectations but in what is.

6.

What lies beyond the noise of the soul is an impenetrable force,
a resounding presence of oneness.

When able to let go and surrender to the unknown you return to the tenderness of life. There can be no true exploration from a place of control. In direct experience you can be free from the illusion of suffering. You have the potential to carry the cradle of life from a place of care. Through this realisation can life be overflowing and abundant in nature. What lies beyond the noise of the soul is an impenetrable force, a resounding presence of oneness. This return brings the potential of being. The highest expression within emanates at a great magnitude. To be in touch with this, the realness of you can be felt. The empowered self and the sense of purpose grows. You do not have to seek purpose for it is already a knowing in the higher self. Such knowing cannot be given from anyone or anything outside of you. In the release of blocks that make you fear yourself the higher aspect of your potential waits.

GUIDANCE   You are not empty, no matter how dark life becomes, how much you are forced to walk alone, when you are ready the grace of life will show itself to you. The journey can be long and the wish to give in and distract yourself strong. This is your test and only you can make the choice to know all parts of you. The treasure that you find along this path is self-belief. Each time you triumph to see truth you are given the sustenance to carry on. To deliver what you are is the learning of how to carry all that is in you. Discovering this is your exploration.

7.

What is real is always new and vital and cannot be rehearsed.

Hiding yourself you close the connection to what is true in you. What is in the heart needs expression for health. Rising emotion seeks expression and can lead you back to the heart essence. To grow the potential in you is to surrender to the inner fire, this intrinsic force that lies in being. You protect in the aim to alleviate yourself from struggle. But to do this you hide the heart away. To hide turns your back on sensitivity and vulnerability. When the heart is open then you deliver what is real and that which leads to brightness. Without this you continue to seek who you really are. What lies in the heart is to be cherished. The heart supports the essence of you. Realising that truth cannot be gained from expectations can free you from what you imagine yourself to be. What is real is always new and vital and cannot be rehearsed. In forgetting what is true is the relearning of how to come to what is real. To open into the higher self, you tread carefully to understand what lies in you.

GUIDANCE   The hardest challenge to empowerment is to let go of knowing. This comes when you have to stop living the image of what you think you should be and to let go of what you think needs to happen. To not know is to let go, to realise you are always being looked after, that life conspires to help you and not to burden you. This trust is lost when you lose inner-knowing, and replace it with the tie of expectation. Inner-knowing comes in the moment when the connection to the heart is open where there is no expectation just direct experience.

8.

When you come from the need to own then you move away from a Holy intent that brings the connection to all living things.

Connection to the super sensitive realm becomes lost when it does not come from direct experience from within. To develop higher consciousness self-belief must be strong. Belief originates from truth and when not cultivated consciously will become weakened. Your potential comes when you create from a higher state of awareness and sensitivity. When you come from the need to own then you move away from a Holy intent that brings the connection to all living things. To be connected, everything has meaning and you are touched by the world around you. Such a reality is uncomplicated and clear. Through the Holy intent pain is banished, for alliance is in all. When this connection is dulled through the shadows of karma then all manner of distractions occur. The fate of the future self lies in the sentiments of that which is created in you today.

GUIDANCE   This knowing does not come from logic but is out of higher sensitivity. To feel peace that comes from freedom delivers this teaching to you. Peace believes in everything and gives life to all. It has nothing to do with what is yours and what is mine. In knowing the Holy expression within can this truth be understood. Each time you are caught in saying this is yours, this is mine, pause and see in your mind's eye yourself giving it away, for this will help dissolve the discord that can build from the sentiments of owning.

9.

The most valued price is to succeed in creating yourself and to find your way to the Holy within.

The delivering of you comes out of managing your path. To free is to deliver out of all that is wished for from the heart and to rise from the inner creative force. From this comes the brightness of you. Seeing truth lays the higher potential. This is realisation of the higher path. The most valued price is to succeed in creating yourself and to find your way to the Holy within. All that is restrictive wants to be freed. To release inner restrictions is a necessary process to go through to be the master of you.

GUIDANCE   Creating yourself is a tentative process that forces you to slow down and be aware of what is happening for you. Uncovering the layers to the true self is a process of remembering your potential. These teachings may feel as if they are far from reach, but that is because you forget the way and not because it is unachievable by you. The Holy is an unmistakable connection. You are no longer lost to the many interpretations of the source of you; you will come in direct union with it and know where you are from. Because we follow we believe the sacred must be delivered through external channels and through chosen people. This belief has rendered us lost and helpless in the self. The Holy waits within you if you wish it.

10.

In the brilliance of your shining do you affect the reality of those around you.

You believe that life needs great effort from you in order to be lived. In this belief you fill yourself with worry and anxiety in order to create. This approach is hard and lays heavy in the heart, for in the higher knowing the experience of life is effortless. Living life undivided without the need to control comes through the true self. When devotion to light becomes reality then life is imbued with the hope of love. To want to expand is a perpetual and natural process. In the brilliance of your shining do you affect the reality of those around you. The higher wish is the return to the core of being.

GUIDANCE   When you lose touch with the core of you it is easy to lose the greater perspective. Interconnectedness is exactly that, you become one with life and the forces of creation. All life exists with the same impulse to grow and expand into all it can be. This is happening to you but also to the whole of the earth. The earth body is also wishing to reach its potential. When you raise your consciousness you have the ability to help raise the consciousness of all around you. As energy forces we affect each other. The earth is a living body that is evolving in its way moving towards its complete state and higher potential. When you come to your higher expression you also help that of the earth to raise its vibration.

11.

To protect, the true nature becomes buried, replaced by a false self to fit in, and this is a hard pain to bear.

To protect, the true nature becomes buried, replaced by a false self to fit in, and this is a hard pain to bear. Life then becomes a task of managing out of that which is not real to you. To learn how to be vulnerable but free is the higher task. When you protect the heart you cannot live that which feels real. The mission is to bring out into life that which is true to you and live it. From here love can be shared and experienced in a higher way. Love comes to those who open in alliance with the creative life force. When you surrender to this union, you surrender to love. Joy becomes manifest without another to create it for you. Love is created from within where the sharing of it is a celebration and not a conditional expression.

GUIDANCE   When someone tells me that they don't know who they are then it can be evident that they live an adapted expression of their true self. Most people live with compromise to their true wish in one way or another. We become locked in to paths we feel we must live and lose our direction. In its extreme we fear being selfish and believe to serve others is a virtue that we must master. Empowerment has no relation to selfishness, compromise or expected virtues. In connection to what moves all of life is what is real, there is no apology or need for validity. This is not a self-centred expression but compassionate and connected. Each time you turn away from your truth you become lost to the higher spirit where you shine.

12.

All pursuits for power externally are illusionary and are created out of discord.

To open to the higher self is no small task. There are many distractions in the world where you now need great attention to turn the focus inwards. When belief and trust is forgotten then there is the need for protection. By losing trust you become exposed and protect yourself from vulnerability. When you feel lost, the sense of belief is weakened. You imagine this has to do with circumstances outside and try to change this to find clarity. All pursuits for power externally are illusionary and are created out of discord. What is important in strengthening the self is to gain belief within. This creates what is real and has an all-encompassing sense of meaning to you. All of creation lives to breathe into its great-ness, to become its limitless self and to allow for all it is. Any restrictions to this flow creates disharmony.

GUIDANCE   When you are not in power then you can drift in life. You have purpose when in alignment with light where direction is found. When we live without purpose you seek to serve something and all too often when the inner world is unfamiliar, you will seek outside of you. Empowerment is the essence of wholeness where you are in touch with the higher aspect, this is everlasting and sustaining. When you are subject to the conditions of gaining or losing power you find that you are not fulfilled. To have fulfilment externally is sustained when you reach this within you first. Balancing your time and finding space for inner exploration is needed for you to tenta-tively grow inner knowing. You find that many distractions will call you away for this channel inwards becomes cluttered and unused. The more you sense within the stronger you will hear your true voice.

13.

Love is the Holy within being.

We release the need for protection when we master and bring ourselves out of fear. There lies a power struggle between what you believe outside and what the innate power is within. In the separation from the true self you ache in the wanting of power. In the wild fight, light endures out of pain. Fear creates borders and limitations where there is the need to protect in order to avoid being vulnerable or over exposed. To hold fast to what you carry in the heart you must take responsibility of yourself. Love is freed out of pain. Love is the Holy within being.

GUIDANCE   Clearing the path of the heart and refining sensitivity will help you to experience the Holy within love. Mastering and opening to super-consciousness is the emanating force of the Holy realised. You believe that you can only reach this place through another but this experience is open to all if they wish it. If this means enough to you and you place attention within then you will reach this dream. What waits for you is your purpose for it comes through the maturity of light where all is understood. Self-realisation is only distant from you if you remain distant to yourself. Being connected means inner knowing from a place that is true. To drive towards this higher wish is your choice. Beginning each day with the intention to not forget to listen to the inner world opens a higher channel that will support this wish. To realise this you must not forget to ask for it.

Summary of Teachings

1. When you rely solely on truth, then you become strengthened to live into the tenderness of the heart, where love is accessed through the power of the creative force.

2. In protecting yourself, you separate from being connected to another and create a divide that fuels judgement and criticism.

3. You invoke protection to shield yourself from pain.

4. Without feeling there is no true connection.

5. Expecting comes from forcing, control and is aggressive by nature.

6. What lies beyond the noise of the soul is an impenetrable force, a resounding presence of oneness.

7. What is real is always new and vital and cannot be rehearsed.

8. When you come from the need to own then you move away from a Holy intent that brings the connection to all living things.

9. The most valued price is to succeed in creating yourself and to find your way to the Holy within.

10. In the brilliance of your shining do you affect the reality of those around you.

11. To protect, the true nature becomes buried, replaced by a false self to fit in, and this is a hard pain to bear.

12. All pursuits for power externally are illusionary and are created out of discord.

13. Love is the Holy within being.

THE IMPACT OF LOSS IS SIGNIFICANT

UNDERSTAND
that the separation from the true self turned
you outwards

LEARN
how the fear of this loss is key to personal
growth

BELIEVE
by facing pain you master reality

1.

Each discord within moves you further away from experiencing the whole self.

In harder moments you learn to fear what lies within and look externally to find resolve. You came to human experience to free all binds to suffering and to experience the true state of being that lies beyond pain. Each discord within moves you further away from experiencing the whole self. The loss of the true state is felt and is now unconsciously longed for and this causes the grief in life. When you free from suffering then the oneness state is reached where you reside in a pure state. Where discord remains you are caught in suffering. To wish to escape grief limits the higher potential and keeps you caught in the cycle of disappointment, despair and longing. In pain is the belief there is no way out. Life is not a punishment but gives the opportunity to come to brightness.

GUIDANCE Our life, our relationships are all healing processes. Through them we learn of how to move the self to greater peace and love. Making the healing process a conscious act places us in the driving seat on our paths. Instead of being taken with the stream of life we have the power to co-create with it. With each resolve is the potential to find meaning and retrieve power. Discord creates charged energies that seek grounding and this is why we feel unsettled and out of balance. We lose connection with a part of the self and this disturbs the equilibrium of how we function. The more we experience discord the further away we go from the meaning and truth that lies within. The capacity to feel love and peace is unlimited in our being and it is only the discord from our wounds that hold us back from living light.

2.

To reach the place of the Holy, the sacred essence of you must be free.

Realising oneness takes you to a state of completion. It is through following the inner path that brings the hope of this return to wholeness. The call in life is asking you to free from following that which is outside of you and to go inside of you. When you stay true to yourself then you begin to live what is real and turn away from blindly following another. You learn to govern yourself. In the return to life is the dreaming to becoming the true self. To reach the place of the Holy, the sacred essence of you must be free. This force asks to know itself through you, you are not separate from it but it is part of you. It is unbound and perfect in its expression and resides beyond all discord. In listening to the inner voice you become brighter. Everything is becoming in life, moving in the way it is designed to. The call is to know what is within you, to be conscious of what you have become and are creating in life.

GUIDANCE   Space is required for you to reach the unlimited aspect. Untethering from pain and releasing all that is not true in you finds this space. Direct experience of the spirit of you cannot be fixed for it comes in a million different ways. It is interpreted but cannot be generalised for this comes from fear and control and does not help you to live into what is true to you. What you think you know of this experience you must let go of, for you cannot know the unknown but respond to it in the moment. This is also true of releasing preconceived ideas of the Holy for this becomes real through direct experience.

3.

Without strengthening inner knowing you live disempowered.

To know what to follow in life you must see what matters to you for what is meaningful comes from the impulses of the heart. Truth is found through feeling. Through feeling you are informed of what is real and what is not. This information allows for the correlation of thought in alignment to sensitivity and this union creates the life you wish to live. By exploring feelings you open to the full spectrum of being. Through reasoning alone you cannot find what you need. Turning outwards to get needs met force you to replace meaning with external constructs and conformities of fear. Without strengthening inner knowing you live disempowered.

GUIDANCE Your intuition is formed from the subtle blend of the many aspects of you. All your senses are taking in messages that move you in one way or another. When someone has strong intuition these messages are moved through the heart bringing about the impulse of a true response. When the heart is not open intuition becomes distorted and finding direction is confusing. It is much rarer than you think to meet people with strong intuition and often these people have been marginalised in some way or have had to live out with society's norms. Power of knowing brings about self confidence that is not shouted about but is integrated as part of you and governs the way you live. Inner knowing is an internal strength that needs no validation. To grow intuition is to return to the heart centre informing you what is meaningful, what lifts you and what doesn't.

4.

Where there is no loss there can be no grief, to experience loss breeds a fear towards the transformative process.

The separation of the true state creates the phenomenon of loss. Where there is no loss there can be no grief, to experience loss breeds fear towards the transformative process. To change, you must come to the edge of what is known in you to see past the illusion of loss. What you know is not what you are. You relate to pain through expectation of what it may bring and are terrified to see the imagined inner void. The consequence of this fear is the fixation that the physical experience is all that exists and this is what you attach to to escape. To face fear is the wish is to break the illusion of grief and loss unto the self. Out of direct experience of facing pain you have the possibility to see that nothing you experience is lost.

GUIDANCE   Through grief we are given the experience to bridge the gap that lies between what we have become and the true self. Without it you are unable to shift into an altered state and revaluate what is meaningful to you. Most people are desperate to get away from grief in the fear you will remain in sorrow. The depth of sorrow mirrors your unique path. The length of time this transformative process can take cannot be measured logically. We come through many lives and each brings sentiments that have created what you carry. Each life is subject to all other lives. It can be common that I witness illness and imbalance following people their whole life. Why is that? In my experience the healing process knows no time. What seems far too long and a waste of a life for some, can for others be what they need to go through in order to release their future self. Spiritual sight is opened when you raise the sensitivity of yourself.

5.

The more the collective experience encourages self-responsibility in transforming the self, the greater the light will manifest in everything.

Taking full responsibility of pain brings perspective to life. Through the healing process you are shown what is being held on to and what needs to be challenged and given up. What is the known must be sacrificed in the face of the unknown. In this offering can blessing be realised. Through this release is offered the beauty of the self. When you touch love with its giving nature and witness that which is in alignment for the highest good, you bring peace. True power lies in the vastness of a free state of being. In running away from fear the opportunity is lost to rise to the higher self. By suppressing or trying to escape from fear you follow the flames of the shadows. You become worn down by the inability to help yourself from struggle and experience shame for the loss of the true self. The more the collective experience encourages self-responsibility in transforming the self, the greater the light will manifest in everything.

GUIDANCE   The wisdom innate in everyone is not a celebrated factor, on a greater scale we are quick to ignore, ridicule, judge or shame another. You believe this is what is needed to succeed. There are many subtle layers in life that this reality is actively promoted. Competitiveness, winning and losing, rewards, gaining, having recognition, validation or to be affirmed are all ways that lose us to the sense of truth within. To help each other actively to be empowered is to support the inner resolve that we all have to go through. This encourages life and frees us from the dullness created from discord.

6.

*Being terrified of facing the void within turns you away from
the true dream.*

The creative life force that resides in you is asking to be free of all the limitations that it endures. When in true power what you wish for becomes real. That is the shining that comes free from inner fire. To give up and lose the fight against fear is common. We don't like to see ourselves vulnerable. Truth is the belief and knowing that in the higher potential there is freedom from all fear. Being terrified of facing the void within turns you away from the true dream. This dream comes out of the uncorrupted self, free and unlimited and is where purpose lies. The higher calling is heard when the heart is open. Navigating fear must be a conscious choice for this higher dream to come into reality.

GUIDANCE It feels challenging to walk away from the crowd, to stand alone and choose to face the unknown in you. You stay attached to the warmth and friendliness of the tribe for the familiarity brings you safety. With breaking free comes doubt and it is the doorway for even more fears to rise. The shadows remain in the dark because you placed them there; they are parts of you that you don't want to see because they do not bring comfort and make you feel safe. This safety does not help you grow but helps you escape your fear. The dream remains in you when you untether the heart and reach that which you have always wished for.

7.

The call is to challenge all that is not in line with your sensitivity where your higher sense of self resides.

The true self is being replaced with what is socially acceptable. A sleep state has been created within out of years of indifference and powerlessness that infiltrate the soul. Where sadness exists there is the higher calling to will the self to go within and regain a true place of shining. In a fallen state inner power still remains waiting to be found. Your innate self never forgets the brightness you hold for it lives in the highest sense of you and it asks for truth to be realised. The tenderness of light cannot be formed from outside. When the world that you create is from inner knowing, then you can live with power without. Creating from truth brings about an invincible will that can drive you to accomplish all you wish. In sensitivity feelings show you the way for the highest good. To experience the tenderness of love you are asked to express all colours without limitation. The call is to challenge all that is not in line with your sensitivity where the higher sense of self resides.

GUIDANCE   Each time you do not allow yourself to feel the way you do you suppress sensitivity. Whenever you find yourself saying I sound stupid, this sounds strange or you can't believe your saying this, these are all subtle ways that you avoid accepting yourself. You side step in order to fit in and not stand apart. Confidence has been knocked many times and this makes you feel inferior or less than others. To regain confidence so that you are able to renew the sense of belief within is to explore your vulnerability. Yes you feel unconfident now but this is a wish to slowly begin to rebuild again. Many people that I work with hide their sensitivity as they see it as a sign of weakness. Learning to see sensitivity in a positive light helps self-belief.

8.

In the expansion of yourself unbound by pain and suffering can the preciousness of life be lived where an even greater exploration waits.

You become a foreigner to yourself. You can create the living dream of bliss that has always been known by you. In the expansion of yourself unbound by pain and suffering can the preciousness of life be lived where an even greater exploration waits. The true self cannot be known through the external reality alone. The fullness of you has to be lived in the truth of the creative life force within. You can transform your outer reality for the highest good.

GUIDANCE   Empowerment is freedom within. Freedom is to love, cry, laugh and to hear your voice and sing its unique song. The potential of life waits for you where each can live by inner-knowing and realise that light is abundant and everlasting. Fear and suffering cannot become a reality when you have this knowing, the knowing that you are connected to everything, that you are light and so is everything else. Bringing this reality to be is in the hands of every one of us, to live into the higher dream. Breaking the illusion of fear lies in seeing it and being conscious of the intention to see what lies beyond it. The magic of life is waiting.

9.

To change discord you re-decide to follow the authority of yourself.

The experience of fear in life exists to propel you forward and to find truth beyond pain. When life lived is created from fear then this becomes how you speak to the world. Each life is the chance to illuminate the self. In each choice there lies the opportunity to create a lighter world for the good of all. In returning to inner knowing is the creation of the self from consciousness. Living from control and self-preservation creates a different reality. The illusion of gaining, achieving and owning is the modern perspective. What you believe in and where you place your attention matters to the life you lead. In truth nothing is here to hold on to and nothing is here to gain. From the place of inner knowing you see that life is not a commodity. You are here to nurture and strengthen the higher qualities and open to the unique expression. In controlling you seek to fixate that which you cannot control. This approach is anti-being and comes from the distortions of modern reality. Following the outer world will not give you the key to your unfolding truth. Many fear the expectation of emptiness if they go within but this is far from what flows through this sacred place of knowing. The collective disorder creates fear towards turning within for it has much to lose. To change discord you re-decide to follow the authority of yourself.

GUIDANCE   You get used to feeling helpless and allow others to lead because it is now the easy option. You do not rock the boat, create friction or put yourself forward for this is the indifference in you. You have long forgotten the strength of life that flows through you. There is no blame, life is evolving this way and we are part of a greater plan. I am aware that you are reading these words which means you have not forgotten, you are feeling the vibration of this book and for some reason it calls to you. This is no coincidence, for this is a book of truth and somewhere in you lies that wish or our paths would not have crossed otherwise. Life is full of miracles, to believe in yourself has already started. It is up to you where you go next with it.

10.

Love begins by speaking to you through the heart, the place of courage where the light of the creator within you resides.

The true state always is in awe of the mystery that flows in life for it is driven from the realness of the heart. This space has the capacity to surprise you. When you become hidden there is an intrinsic knowing of this suppression within the self. Inner knowing is powerful and it is the higher intelligence that never sleeps. Love begins by speaking to you through the heart, the place of courage where the light of the creator within you resides. In the acceptance of all that you are you bring this light to life. You cannot speculate or theorise on the realms of the inner world for it is the unchartered territory that must be witnessed by direct connection. To master the self from a place of control or premeditated ideas means you are working out of a distorted part of you. That which is careful from within does not come from a place of force but from a place where the heart is alleviated from the need to control. No one has more or less than another, we cannot compare worth or value with another. When you surrender to all that you are and move beyond fear then that which is still to be explored within is vast.

GUIDANCE   You become trapped when you search for love outside of you. Love is present as a state of being and not as a conditioned state. To love another means that the heart has opened for that person, but you did not acquire love from them it was always there in you. To realise the state of oneness is love, a sustaining force that is not switched on and off but remains as a constant reality. Love is not attached and does not need another to be. When you suffer in loss you believe that something has been taken away. In truth this is a belief that you have made your reality for you have lost nothing.

11.

In wanting is a constant fear of loss for what we believe we have, we do not want to lose.

You become caught in wanting of life, attaching to desire. In wanting is a constant fear of loss for what we believe we have, we do not want to lose. Through this attachment is created a subtle aggression. Hardship follows in wanting. This is the challenge, to move past the pressures of desire and disappointment created out of fear. In demanding from life you lose touch with truth. Where there is complacency in life, we become defensive. By living out of limited means we accept the present reality as it is. The intervention of this is the return to light, to be in connection to what is lost in you. The hallowed presence cannot exist in a place of discord; you must first release that which binds you. To dream of the brilliance of you comes from the co-creation of being. Supreme consciousness within is reached beyond the sentiments of force and control. Empowerment lies within the transcendence of desire and self-preservation.

GUIDANCE   The impulse to wish for something is natural, this is not what is in question but when the desire is delivered from discord you will find that you attach to this goal. Anxiety or expectation forces you to worry for you make this desire out to be of great value. The peace in you has no need to control and so where there lays little peace, you become trapped in external wanting. Understanding what motivates you is key to breaking this pattern. Remind yourself that when something does not come to you even though you desired it strongly is because it is not what you really need but something else waits for you. To forget that another door is opening that you cannot see right now forces you to fixate on what you want at any cost. This is learning to let go and remember that what you are really wishing for comes but not always in the way you think it will.

12.

Loss symbolises the broken union to the true self.

There is the feeling of being overwhelmed by suffering. Where life could be effortless, it is not, and becomes replaced with struggle. By asking only of the external world a rift is created between the true self and the outer self. In oneness there is unconditional completeness where you rely on nothing but what comes from you. Living from the separateness of being creates a distorted image of you. Sacrifice has been part of a Holy fight for you believe you have to give up all that you are to live truth. The task is to overcome fear and learn from the teachings that are unique to you and the life you live. The phenomenon of loss is created in the wake of this separation. Loss symbolises the broken union to the true self.

GUIDANCE   Loss is created from discord, a distortion of you. It is like a trap that we fall into, it holds us there because we have lost this truth within us. The authenticity of being is filled with light for there is no discord here. What you receive through the interconnectedness within is this reflected to you externally. Life becomes effortless when you have this understanding. To deliver the true self comes with no fear of loss. Joining into the oneness of being comes through the connectedness of all parts of you. In the acceptance of who you are, what you have become and the will to know yourself deeper releases you from the illusion of loss.

13.

Life calls you to feel your abundance again, to fear nothing and to embrace the fountain of power within.

In the return to oneness the sovereign state sustains you. The wish of achieving this higher purpose becomes lost when you turn outwards. Pain and suffering is created through the desire of achievement when you do not feel complete within. Life calls you to feel abundance again, to fear nothing and to embrace the fountain of power within. That which is the true self expresses itself differently to the expectations created in modern culture. The sadness of life exists from the inner knowing that life is being lived through a distorted version of what you truly are. Your creative fire cannot flourish with such constraints. That which has permeated within as loss exists because it is believed in and you follow this reality, not light.

GUIDANCE   Trusting yourself is to reveal and accept all of you in an honest way. You become restricted by the internal borders of resistance, the desire to be something that you may not be. We can create false lives because we feel that way inside. If belief is not strong you become unstable and will call to another for validation. Opening comes from seeing without the mask. Yes this is a tentative process and no one asks you to rush this. To ignore yourself is the detriment to us all. Each time someone is empowered we all feel it. Because it comes from love its impulse is life giving. The ability to show is brought about by constant practice, to find quiet spaces to hear yourself. Take time through your day to pause and remember to be aware of what is touching you. To awaken the dream of the potential in you is a constant battle and this path needs much reminding. It is not how you do it but that you do not forget to do it.

Summary of Teachings

1. Each discord within moves you further away from experiencing the whole self.

2. To reach the place of the Holy, the sacred essence of you must be free.

3. Without strengthening inner knowing you live disempowered.

4. Where there is no loss there can be no grief, to experience loss breeds a fear towards the transformative process.

5. The more the collective experience encourages self-responsibility in transforming the self, the greater the light will manifest in everything.

6. Being terrified of facing the void within turns you away from the true dream.

7. The call is to challenge all that is not in line with your sensitivity where your higher sense of self resides.

8. In the expansion of yourself unbound by pain and suffering can the preciousness of life be lived where an even greater exploration waits.

9. To change discord you re-decide to follow the authority of yourself.

10. Love begins by speaking to you through the heart, the place of courage where the light of the creator within you resides.

11. In wanting is a constant fear of loss for what we believe we have, we do not want to lose.

12. Loss symbolises the broken union to the true self.

13. Life calls you to feel your abundance again, to fear nothing and to embrace the fountain of power within.

FOLLOW THE WISDOM OF YOURSELF

UNDERSTAND
with self-belief you do not need to change
another to validate you

LEARN
what you have become is your creation and you
can recreate yourself

BELIEVE
the external world cannot bring the security
you wish for

1.

When self-belief is aligned with the true essence you will not need to alter another person's belief to validate yourself.

You live by who you are and what you believe in. All choices are in your hands, for all that you create comes from your making. The higher task is in creating you. How you live drives all pain and happiness. What is wished for is your choice, when truth is not followed within you will seek to follow those outside. What lives inside of you cannot be like any other for you are a unique being. How you live the experience of life cannot be compared to how another lives theirs. Your story is yours; the way you see and respond is authentic to you, to know this you must see what lies within. To get lost in comparing or judging to another is just a distraction. To surrender to the unknown within brings self-belief. Your belief is yours regardless if another associates with it or not. When self-belief is aligned with the true essence you will not need to alter another person's belief to validate yourself.

GUIDANCE   When you believe in something the effect it has on the way you create life is powerful. Imagine a tree with its main tap root that anchors it solidly into the ground. Its purpose is not just to feed the tree but to give it stability against the changing influences of the weather. This is like belief, it is the foundation of you, without it external influences can wash over you, overwhelm you, de-root you and knock you down. From this instability you will search to find other people to make you feel solid again and this becomes the validation that you will need constantly. Inner knowing creates self-belief; and has strength and power to withstand any storm.

2.

You stray from the path when you follow another's truth over
your own for this comes from you alone.

When you rely on another, this is a temporary crutch. You stray from the path when you follow another's truth over your own for this comes from you alone. To deliver the authentic self is to open to all that you are without justification or resistance. In fear you hold on to another. In the fall from truth you become overshadowed by fear. Even with fear you have to make choices in life. Believing that hope comes out of another's expression does not stay true to who you are. Belief formed from following another comes out of the fear within. To have self-belief you must look at what comes up in you. There is collective belief that there can be no other way but to support this perspective of following. To come into the higher aspect is to manage out of belief. Freedom and the dream of the higher potential come's when you turn inwards. This is the surrendering to your fire.

GUIDANCE   You can get lost in the formalities and conditioning of life. You become indifferent to those who lead you and are in authority because you believe they know more than you. This is a subtle conditioning that gives power away. I do not promote rebellion and the creation of further tyrannies but the knowledge that to truly change reality to one that emanates truth and freedom you cannot follow blindly. Truth is reliant on you to be conscious of what you are experiencing and be the authority of yourself. This is what matters, if you feel uneasy, troubled or uncomfortable this is what is real to you and you must listen to this and have the courage to let it lead you.

3.

*In the wisdom of life, you are given all that you need to
complete yourself.*

To face what you have become is to free from the illusion
of pain. By not facing pain you are unable to reach the higher
lesson that it is trying to show you. The wisdom in discomfort comes to teach you what you need to help you grow and
expand into an even greater potential. You learn why pain
comes and what you need from it to grow. Truth is the understanding of your experience of life and from here you grow
the inner knowing. Uncovering truth strengthens self-belief.
Each time you face pain or fear lays the potential for self-
belief to become stronger. Belief is the knowing that grows
empowerment. In the wisdom of life, you are given all that
you need to complete yourself. What is real is reached when
there is freedom from the restrictions you place within you.

GUIDANCE   The answers are all in you; this is not a cliché
but a truth waiting to be seen by you. There is no knowledge,
discipline or practice that can alter the potential of you, it is
already there. The miracle through the healing process reveals
that you hold all the keys to higher development regardless
of what you are shown. The essence of you is desperate to
breathe its truth, to have space to express itself without the
limitations. This is not being indulgent or selfish but unlocks
true power that loves and is connected to all. Following what
is in the heart brings you to the higher calling; the task is to
remember to listen to the heart again.

4.

*The true fight is not the battle outside of you but to surrender
to what is real within for this leads to the victory
of empowerment.*

Proving yourself to another brings only conditional happiness. The pursuit for external happiness is temporary and is an illusion to real happiness. The true fight is not the battle outside of you but to surrender to what is real within for this leads to the victory of empowerment. Instead of settling for what you believe you should be remember to give attention inwards. You are learning to stand apart, to face the task that is the way within. In surrendering you can let go of your dependency on others to make you feel whole. In defeat you hold on to another to manage what is lacking within. The sorrow in the heart becomes heavy and the fight overwhelming. The task is to bring the fire and to set it free from the pain that oppresses you. To heal the masks you wear is to surrender to what lays beyond fear and pain, for through this waits joy.

GUIDANCE   You give attention to the struggles externally, the worry of relationships, fulfilment at work, what you have and what you don't have. To fix or fight to bring about harmony in the outer reality is an endless task. What this teaching shows is that when you have the courage to let go of holding on to these power struggles outside of you, your life will change. The fear of trying to continually control the outer reality is a trap that you have fallen into. Trust comes out of knowing the abundant nature of inner creativity. It is to realise that in worry and fear you solve nothing. Harmony cannot be created out of fear. Find the peace inside of you and watch the external reality change towards peace in a natural way.

5.

Meaning cannot be created when you become numb.

To have wisdom you must break free from the safety of what you know and expect. Loosening the grip of controlling life opens you to truth. Through direct insight lies the ability to overcome what is limiting you. Courage is now needed to navigate life's experiences consciously. The hardship in life has worn truth. You become lost in grief and sadness in the recovery process. Hope comes when the meaning to pain and suffering is found within. Meaning cannot be created when you become numb. What lies beyond pain is freedom from grief and sadness. Creative awakening is led by the movement of emotion. Grace and acceptance of all that you are comes when you let go of forced control. To love openly with courage is from the heart where you access dreams and wishes. Trusting the wisdom of emotions is key to the higher potential.

GUIDANCE   It can take years to steadily open trust in you again. You become numb for good reason. If the path you have lived has been overwhelming for your sensitivity you will shut down to feeling for this was a necessary safety for you. Accepting that this is a difficult journey is important to all of us for we are continually learning and growing. In the wish of the heart you can ask for that opening and when you don't forget even if you are not ready now one day you will be. We are always growing and evolving, we are not perfect and if you fool yourself that you are then this construct keeps you stuck. Your opening is like a dear friend returning to your life, it brings relief. Go carefully and seek the support you need and you can release the pain you carry.

6.

Everyone is creating and what you are creating is in your hands.

To live truth is the learning of forgiveness of you. Forgiveness releases the struggle of pain in being. You are not here to suffer but to free into light. Forgiveness allows you to accept all that you are and this sets you free from the pain of suffering. Surrendering to inner life brings the meaning you are looking for, for here you accept truth and this is a step to empowerment. Opening keeps you following the path that is right for you. Pain is a transitory feeling, with resolve it will disperse and when you feel through it you become fearless. Pain is only as frightening as you believe it is. With belief and strength you can disperse its effect on you. Everyone is creating and what you are creating is in your hands. To not forget and to strengthen the will of yourself moves you to brightness.

GUIDANCE   These teachings do not come from a place of criticism or judgement in fact they celebrate the being and the greatness of you. But truth is not sentimental or wants to impress you. It is the higher knowing that comes from the universal origins of life. Man's creation of life is often far removed from these higher truths. They remind you of something you have forgotten. In your hands is free will and that you deliver light. To bring about change in life is your responsibility. To hide the heart makes life into a hard and limited reality. Through opening again you free the prayer in the heart and open to the greater aspects of being. Peace comes inevitably when you create consciously from what has meaning to you.

7.

The human fire is the expression of the highest good.

The human fire is the expression of the highest good. When you move away from the true self pain is created. To follow the wisdom within is to learn to trust. To not hide but to live naked regains the true essence of you. To follow another will not create you in the truest way. Corruption in the self seeks ways to cheat life and become lost in desire and torment. The drama of life becomes the spectacle that you become distracted too and so little is meaningful. The sense of separation and individualism has made you distant from the wholeness of living. In the avoidance of the self is the rise of temptation for external gain. When corruption and indifference fills life, then what you stand for has little meaning. The solution for pain in life is sought in external comfort and gain. The myth is that you are cast into oblivion, to search endlessly for the unanswerable questions. You believe that a high price must be paid in order to reach the higher goal. You do not have to endlessly search for truth, you already have it inside of you. What is sought waits within.

GUIDANCE   What serves you is not always what feels comfortable. People are unsure to follow that which brings true meaning in the heart. There is a belief that to follow the heart is an idealistic and self-centred distraction. For life to be lived in its potential this is an illusion we must break as we are being asked to embrace the light and the dark aspects of our self. Listening to the impulse of how you feel about things matters. For example the heart may spring with joy at the thought of meeting someone who makes you feel light and this becomes something that you listen to. Then as you develop the relationship you notice that you begin to feel uncomfortable and experience heavy impulses. Sticking to something that repeatedly does not feel good sabotages you. Following the heart does not mean discomfort will not follow but it is to have awareness to how you are responding and listen to that. What matters is to know the sensitivity of you is ever changing and informing you. You cannot know what you will feel but be present to see the realness in you and accept it.

8.

You fear following what is in you because of the belief that nothing will come and that you are empty of anything real.

You are helped to let go of holding on to external sources when you find the wisdom of truth. Freedom lies in creating out of sovereignty without following or attaching to another. What is created in life is what you wish for. You are looking to understand the findings of sensitivity and to learn to choose out of this. This is the training of the power of will within.

You must have the desire to grow you. To align all choices to what you believe is to live a higher way. You fear following what is in you because of the belief that nothing will come and that you are empty of anything real. Following others causes you to fall far from the true state of being. When you attach to what is outside, you encourage the void within and believe only in external security.

GUIDANCE   When you get so used to endless distractions, information and influences from outside, you become very full. This feeling brings you a false security of being part of something even if in truth you are merely sitting on the fence regarding your potential. You cannot compete with these distorted processes that you know as reality, it is a losing game. You imagine that you can keep integrity in tact when all that you immerse in comes from discord. You imagine the sorrow of having to leave the safety of what you know and hold on even more to these distractions. This can be why it feels so hard to turn inwards. It can feel like a loss. This is the emptiness that you are imagining but as with all grief this is the letting go process that is inevitable. Many have walked this path and know of the pitfalls. Do not let the fear of emptiness stop you from going within for sooner or later you will see this is not true. The abundant nature of being waits behind this illusion.

9.

To open to what lies in the heart is to accept both sorrow and joy alike, for you cannot favour one over the other in order to grow.

Following others creates treason in you. To surrender and to let go is your decision. Choices are yours to make in creating life. Separating from the brightness within makes you forget who you are and the potential of you. Every choice is orchestrated by you and when you make a choice directed from truth then the path becomes lighter. To stand alone in light is a feared task. What is real in the self has become alien to you and has been modified and distorted. To open to what lies in the heart is to accept both sorrow and joy alike for you cannot favour one over the other in order to grow. To accept parts of you and not others creates division and you are learning to break this illusion.

GUIDANCE   How to accept all processes in you without resistance or division is the question. If you don't like something you resist it and priorities what is agreeable to you over that which is not. You don't want to feel bad, discomfort or vulnerable this is common to us all. We actively encourage a reality that supports suppressing and taking discomfort away at all cost regardless of the implications of its impact on our soul development. Until you have the conviction to say no to these paths the others cannot open to you. It is not for you to fix what comes next but to trust that following truth carves a lighter path ahead. To know it is to do it for only you have the power to create your reality.

10.

*To know the extent of light, you must know the extent
of darkness.*

Many have moved away from their original blue print of
being. What was unique in you became distorted. Life is
conspiring to help you move to the perfect expression of you.
This remains the highest calling, to return to the true expression of you. In the higher self there is no need to control and
manipulate life to suit your expectations. The creative life
force is always new, vital and informed; it is in all life and
is accessed through the heart. You build castles with high
walls to protect you from all that feels out of your control.
You create a divide between you and the rest of life. To know
the extent of light, you must know the extent of darkness. By
knowing the opposite expression you learn the higher lessons
of life. Through experiencing inhibition and control, you are
learning to live the promise of the liberated self. This dynamic
is created to serve you and not to disempower you.

GUIDANCE   Often we will want to speak of light and
empowerment more than the shadows of life. We struggle to
find a common language to healing and knowing that pain is
truth. We view illness and suffering as a dark force that we do
not want to know. We hide these parts of our self in the knowing
that others are frightened too. To turn this perspective around
life asks us to embrace that which frightens us, to see that it
has as much value as light. Becoming is the transcendence of
light and dark to realise beyond these polarities. Joy comes
when you see past the illusion of how you have been created.

To do this we must find balance to not run away from the self but have faith in the strength of human nature. The collective experience of the shadows in life is feared and a belief that you need saving because you are incapable of managing yourself promotes a powerless state. You do not need to fear yourself or your life; to live it is to find the way through.

11.

In the sovereignty of being, you do not try to be anything you believe you should be, for you follow no image of yourself.

In the higher realm nothing masks your essence and you are able to express your true purpose. What is real for you creates a strong energy and is clear in the world. In the sovereignty of being you do not try to be anything you believe you should be for you follow no image of yourself. You do not want; for all searching is over and all need for another to affirm you is unnecessary. When the Holy within becomes lost then self-belief is weak and you forget the brightness of being. Out of inner knowing you do not need to follow another, for no one can get your light but you.

GUIDANCE   Doubt has followed the image of man for a long time. Treason has enveloped the consciousness of truth yet still the resilience of light remains. What serves you is now, what lives within is your showing. You believe you can't follow yourself because others cannot show you what this looks like. You do not gain sovereignty from comparing or being led. There is no map, manual or script. Each of us stands alone in the great mystery of our self and our relationship to creation is our unfolding. The sovereignty of your power is not a force that is apart from the world, but is very much living as one with it. The challenge is to be with the struggle of life and still open the heart within it.

12.

In every choice is the possibility to live into the brightness of being and to free yourself from all that weighs you down.

For empowerment, you train the mind to be in relationship with the heart. To express yourself from thought alone creates limitations to how you see yourself and how you behave. When you are able to create in alignment with the heart, the mind is free to serve what you believe in. You become trapped when you follow what others think you should be, creating further suffering. The mind is a powerful ally and must be harnessed for freedom to exist. In every choice is the possibility to live into the brightness of being and to free yourself from all that weighs you down.

GUIDANCE   Think of a choice you need to make, for example, do I take this job or not? Sit or lie comfortably and place the hands on the heart. Be there until you can feel the rhythm of the heart and relax into the soothing rise and fall of the chest. Now observe the response of your sentiments. This means the way your body sensations move and the heart feels. Now when you recall the choice you ask yourself is this choice right for you? If you feel uplifted, strong and open this shows you that energy flows within you. To feel the lightness reinforces a strong Yes showing you that this is the right decision for you. If you feel overcome with stress or tension within, feel nothing or heaviness then this is a No. To put this into practice you can start by using the bigger choices you have to make and then move on to the smaller ones. The challenge lies in following your response through. Even when you doubt yourself have the courage to follow what you see and this way you grow your sensitivity and connection to the higher self.

13.

Learning to create from your making is the wisdom of you.

In modern life it is hard to know what is real. You prove to yourself and not to another. Through your way, you feel free. What you become is created by you, which means you have the power to recreate what is in you. Learning to create from your making is following the wisdom of you. Reliance within cannot come from those around you. Following the wisdom in you transforms reality. In sacred union is the higher potential reached. This transformation is available to all, where the dream of oneness can be realised. Life is created unconditionally and free, this is known in the higher self. Until this reality comes to fruition you continue to return to life to seek it. In the highest state of being is the Holy. In this place resides the sacred. Its consciousness is life giving, eternal and loving. To live from here is to experience no separation from within. Free from shadows of the self you find your kingdom, where honour, joy and peace reside.

GUIDANCE   We attach wisdom to someone who carries perspective, places truth above sentimentality and is able to believe with conviction what they know. Wisdom is universal in nature and reflects the interconnectedness of human nature. We love to hear wisdom because it is light and clear in its presentation. Wisdom lies within you and is accessible no matter the status, rank or experience. Wisdom does not know its own value but is accepting. Life void of wisdom becomes barren and heartless, for the food of the soul is carried in wisdom. Joining the parts of yourself and moving to wholeness comes from how you create in life and the way you understand yourself. To live your truth is your choice, and this is the celebration of life.

What has been will be again.

Summary of Teachings

1. When self-belief is aligned with the true essence you will not need to alter another person's belief to validate yourself.

2. You stray from the path when you follow another's truth over your own for this comes from you alone.

3. In the wisdom of life, you are given all that you need to complete yourself.

4. The true fight is not the battle outside of you but to surrender to what is real within for this leads to the victory of empowerment.

5. Meaning cannot be created when you become numb.

6. Everyone is creating and what you are creating is in your hands.

7. The human fire is the expression of the highest good.

8. You fear following what is in you because of the belief that nothing will come and that you are empty of anything real.

9. To open to what lies in the heart is to accept both sorrow and joy alike for you cannot favour one over the other in order to grow.

10. To know the extent of light, you must know the extent of darkness.

11. In the sovereignty of being you do not try to be anything you believe you should be for you follow no image of yourself.

12. In every choice is the possibility to live into the brightness of being and to free yourself from all that weighs you down.

13. Learning to create from your making is the wisdom of you.

IV

YOUR EMPOWERMENT

You Have A Life And A Purpose

UNDERSTAND
why you fear your higher potential

LEARN
how to change reality in order to serve you

BELIEVE
that you are responsible for your life

1.

Purpose lies in the maturity of your light, for this is the pride of your existence where you integrate the higher self into life.

When in wholeness you have the potential to radiate magnificent colours. Without empowerment within you are forced to reconcile your needs another way. The dynamic between the true self and what is false from within, creates a driving force to re-finding the inner path. You become distracted in the pursuit of external achievement. To find the inner path you must be prepared to not follow another, but to come within and take responsibility of what you carry. To have peace, you cannot blame another or escape from all that you are but learn how to accept pain. Seeing all your colours, you learn how to re-create reality to serve your higher potential that is unbound and free. The loss of integrity is created from the absence of truth which creates discord. Beyond suffering lies the greatness of love. Conforming has been the safe option where there is little self-belief. You turn rigid and hard from the demands placed upon you when you follow others. When you become lost to the higher aspect of you, this dulls the true meaning of purpose. Purpose lies in the maturity of your light, for this is the pride of existence where you integrate the higher self into life.

GUIDANCE   Inner knowing is active when you live into the higher purpose. Distractions, helplessness and the poverty of life is no longer a reality for you. Each time you grow light the more fills your being. We are energy. Through the healing process managing the energy of discord feels a constant battle. This can be done in many ways and here are but a few, by reading uplifting and life giving texts, listening to higher vibrational music, placing healing objects in the home, walks in nature, yoga, cleansing and grounding practices, breathing exercises, placing images around you that are full of light and hope, and the list goes on. To heal you can be moved through dark spaces. Being proactive in filling the heart with light from external sources lightens the burden.

2.

With self-knowledge and sensitivity belief is strong, where you break the ties from suffering and corruption.

To open to your higher state, your fragile nature must be seen. To live carefully is to become conscious and aware of what you are becoming. Without awareness you become drawn back into the drama of discord. You have courage to walk into the unknown. Through surrendering you come to inner-knowing. The seed of hope comes from peace within and is beyond all the labours of this world. In the hallowed presence is the counter force to suffering in the world. The Holy lies beyond fear and banishes pain. When the brightness of you shines then power struggles cease. All pain becomes transient. With self-knowledge and sensitivity belief is strong, where you break the ties from suffering and corruption.

GUIDANCE   There is a part of you that remembers that life comes with no effort, that suffering is not the reality and hardship merely an illusion. Hope comes through truth and the joining to the higher frequency of you. You are not tied to anything, but free. These teachings are shared to remind you of what has always been known. The tragedy for life was you forgot. To remember again is to ignite the will to be relentless in the pursuit of freedom. When there is hope then this affects everyone around you. Take a moment of each day to remember this higher potential, read it, hear it or see it, do it your way for there lies many traps that will encourage you to forget.

3.

By escaping into the external reality, you lose power.

Trying to escape suffering perpetuates fear. Where fear exists then joy cannot. In the true self, joy is revealed through surrendering to the inner fire. The true self becomes weakened because of being answerable to karmic processes. By escaping into the external reality, you lose power. Belief within the wholeness of being is to live no separation within. The higher wisdom that lies in you is mighty and life will seek out to balance you towards higher truth. The natural flow of expression in the world moves freely when the noise of the soul quietens. Purpose is found through life unfolding from a felt sense.

GUIDANCE   Your power lies in what you believe in. When you follow another, whether an individual or the collective, you are still searching for your power. The danger here is that you imagine that empowerment is to do with a self-centred detachment from the world. This is not the case. Truth is love and where there is no love there is discord. You stand alone when in the sovereignty of being but you remain one with life. Direct experience of truth cannot be given to you by another. To be present is to allow life to enter you and be one with it and see your response to it without fear of where it takes you. Being alert to yourself and the environment can also exist for the purpose of exploration of life.

4.

You have not been given an impossible task for you have evolved to this point and possess all you need to face the fears inside of you.

When there is separation from the true self you will live with expectations externally. Life becomes lived in a mapped out way and you become caught in the race of time. Your truth cannot come out of a time bound reality for this is restricting. Feeling separated from within places enormous pressure on you in the world. When you let go of control life will not fall apart, you are an ever-moving and unlimited force. In the circumstances that you were born in, you already have with you what you need to grow. You are conditioned to reject, fight and manipulate life. From fear you resist surrendering to all that you have become. Vulnerability contains the beauty of your being, for through it lies truth. The reason for your incarnation is to live through the events and happenings that are on your path, with the heart open. You have not been given an impossible task, for you have evolved to this point and possess all you need to face the fears inside of you. You cannot compare your experience with another, for this is your journey alone.

GUIDANCE We tend to focus on what is lacking in life and so forget to remember this higher teaching. Believing that you cannot do something or have the ability to manage has been decided by you but is not a truth. The spiritual realm mirrors that the events and circumstances that come to you are no mistake. You are not a victim of your life only if you choose to be. Accepting this is the healing journey. When you can understand the higher reasons why something comes to show you what you need to learn, then you realise truth is in you. Becoming is this journey where taking responsibility means accepting the story of the life you have, and learning to embrace who you are.

5.

The Holy lives as the highest source of being and your potential lies in the realisation of it.

To live from the lower forces of the soul, you become governed by its will. Understand that the healing of fear is essential for growth. Through this challenge you learn to master yourself. When the heart becomes relieved of its suffering, this makes way for love to thrive. If you become over shadowed in the soul, the more you become blind to love. The Holy lives as the highest source of being and your potential lies in the realisation of it. In your hands is the choice to grow light or diminish it. In direct experience of the highest source in you, is belief and faith. When life is created without masks then there is freedom from all that is inhibiting you.

GUIDANCE   To know the Holy aspect of you comes from inside of you. When you follow another person's version of it this can only take you so far in envisioning this truth. At some point or other you will come to your own realisation. This is the evolutionary path. How long it takes you to get there is not of great importance as this journey will take the time that all aspects of your being need to be ready. Joining into oneness where you live in light aligned with the higher self is not predetermined by you. Our lives are mere preparations for this awakening and what happens next cannot be predicted. To be ready is to refine yourself and the grace of God will come. Strengthening your being, and living truth is this preparation, for you must be ready to hold the intensity of this light.

6.

It's important to support each other and not condemn the natural process of healing.

To expect and predetermine in life blocks you from living your true purpose. Through hardship the passion for life becomes lost to indifference. The spirit of being is dampened by constructs of the mind that try to control and fixate. In doing so limitations are created to what you really came for. Letting go of control allows you to see life for what it really is and to respond to it. To control comes from fear and is entangled in the shadows of the self. It's important to support each other and not condemn the natural process of healing. To help release pain, disharmony or disease you are being called to go within. To have courage to see your shadow, loosens the grip of control and slowly you become free of the limitations within. In answering this call is the chance to reinstate integrity of being. Witnessing the story of your soul brings self-belief and power back. Seeing the weave of life in you is what delivers the real self.

GUIDANCE   It is a distorted reality when we put each other down instead of empowering each other. This happens when insecurity fills the heart and the weight of this brings you down. It becomes inevitable that you will sooner or later do the same to another. How we treat each other is the mirror of how we treat our self. If internally you criticise, punish and hurt yourself you will do it to others. Because we are all sentient beings we will always affect each other. A way that helps us to not shame or punish our self for the hard thoughts we have, is to counteract this distorted energy with conscious compassion. In prayer or mediation each night tell yourself that you are healing and that all the discord inside of you is not part of your true being. Forgive this state and wish that no harm comes to another. This has a peaceful counter effect on the negative energy that can accumulate from discord.

7.

When you cannot accept yourself then dissatisfaction in your external life continues.

Trying to control life creates the pressures of modern work. The main aspect of this pressure comes from want for more. When you cannot accept yourself then dissatisfaction in the external life continues. In the true essence of the self one is love, complete and whole, seeking for nothing more than you are. Modern life creates extreme conditions and comes from the despair of discord. This monotony creates a sleep state within and distracts you from creating space to live consciously and responsibly. When you create from inner knowing very different impulses can be experienced than that of the unconscious self. In oneness life becomes a co-creative process where you do not create further division internally. In consciousness the carefulness of you is awakened and this is light.

GUIDANCE   Without acceptance, the life you lead will never seem enough. The instinctual need for more comes when there is no peace within. True peace is all sustaining. It does not just come when you have what you desire and then go as you wait for the next goal to be achieved. Peace is a state of being not a transitory process. Because of the powerful drive to give attention to what's created in the outer world you lose touch with what is real in you. The belief that when you get that new job or a new car that you will feel complete cannot truly fulfil you. You tie yourself in knots for the frustration that will come from this. You seek to satisfy desire not because it means something real to you but because it provides a distraction from the deep frustration that you hold in yourself. The battle is not outside, but to find the patience and courage to move past the dense energy of frustration in you, and see what you are really dissatisfied with.

8.

You will experience resistance within and also through the collective consciousness.

Sensitivity is strengthened through the engagement and exploration of your inner world. From heaviness created in the heart, fear accumulates. With fear you experience the feeling of imminent danger and being exposed. You will experience resistance within and also through the collective consciousness. People make an enemy of feeling. It is of service to you to train carefully in order to regain a true perspective of the higher state within. When you create from the true self, purpose will come. To embrace the creative life force, the wish of completion can be realised. This higher wish has always been there, to return to the higher calling and to bring this in to the physical world.

GUIDANCE   Most of popular culture is driven towards giving an impression of success, happiness and wealth. Such attributes divide society, create hierarchies and authority figures. This happens out of the need to escape the darker shades of what is created in the world. People place a stigma towards what is dark or bad, and fuel the resistance to it.

You focus only on what is pleasurable and learn to walk away from what discomforts you. Joy and pain now compete, but neither one is the true state. You cannot know true joy until you experience the complete self, and so you remain chasing the image of what you or the collective have projected happiness to be. To stand apart is to question if what comes towards you in life resonates with your truth, and then bypass the borders that keep you trapped. For example when you next feel that you are intuitively drawn to something, or someone that everyone else believes is wrong, are you still able to follow this?

9.

The cream of life, the fullness of being, comes from emersion in your inner world, and following that which is true to you.

In grief you seek to fill the void that is left within. Disempowerment comes when you move away from your inner process. Out of despair you are lost to endless distractions outside of you. The cream of life, the fullness of being, comes from the emersion in your inner world, and following that which is true to you. To be given that crowning, you must stay true to exploring what is real for you beyond all other external influences. From the higher expression you grow true perspective. By navigating back carefully you join the higher cause. In turning outwards you blindly follow others and a state of lament is created within. The greatness of you is feared and you fall to the desire for external gain. You are bound to life processes until consciousness of the true self is realised. Life on earth gives the perfect conditions for you to reach your higher potential.

GUIDANCE   Inside you are so rich and yet you become lost to the riches outside of you. People describe to me that they cannot see where they are going. All emphasis is placed on their external path. It is common place to only look outside for the answers. Few want to hear that for true change to happen, they may have to let go of the reality they know and feel safe in. These teachings have to be integrated slowly as to abandon the life you have lived for so long will not serve you either. I am reminded regularly in healing that there is no quick fix. There are many layers to growing and you must see that healing is life and not separate to it. Believing that the inner life is something that only is looked at as a last resort is counter-productive to opening and going higher. The pursuit of happiness lies in inner truth. Your response to what you read, hear or sense is what is real for you in this moment, and this will continue to inform the next moment.

10.

Your life force seeks for joy and beauty effortlessly, for her creation is the essence of all impulses.

Experiencing the inner self means you cannot fix it in anyway, for it is ever moving. Instead of co-creating you flow against the creative force within. Life is an endless expression of becoming. Holding on to, controlling or trying to form life, limits you. Light is indefinite in character, ever changing and ever growing. Being conscious comes from the union to the creative life force that illuminates the path ahead, for it is the brightness of you. Your life force seeks for joy and beauty effortlessly, for her creation is the essence of all impulses. When you are not in wholeness you are held back from the beauty of this knowing. To live your purpose, you must move past suffering and realise the creative being that lies within. In you is the choice to walk towards power or to diminish it.

GUIDANCE   If you try to understand the creative force through control, fixating what you believe it should be, you will never get close to it, for this is life's mystery. The mind strives for unobtainable perfect conditions, but you forget your origins that you are not perfectly ordered. Life is ever expansive and free. The connection to this force delivers you to a true state. It is this part of you that you feel your inner knowing from. Even a library of books would not be able to hold the vastness of knowledge that comes with you. In pain you dampen this connection for it moves through the heart of you. When the heart is closed so is the impulse of this inner knowing. Coming back is the remembering, and unlocking this comes through creating the space you need to open, and to not forget.

11.

You chose this reality; you chose the earth beyond all other realities for realisation and to then go beyond this.

In today's reality time and space creates many challenges. How you live matters for this is what creates your reality.

Your unique expression wants to experience itself on earth. You chose this reality; you chose the earth beyond all other realities for realisation and to then go beyond this. The brightness of you is wishing for its realisation and to bring about the supreme self. To accomplish this you must move through the shadows of yourself and be ready to realise the magnitude of being. You are not a passenger of life, you are responsible for it. By being here, the unique design and wisdom of the earth gives the exact circumstances for you to reach the Holy essence within. Through lifetimes of making choices you are living to realise yourself free.

GUIDANCE   We feel we don't have a choice; we want to believe that this is all some cosmic hardship and that we are merely being taken for a ride. We look for endless explanations to prove to our self a terrible conspiracy has brought our downfall. These endless stories mean nothing to the higher evolutionary state, they merely distract you. You want to believe that all the suffering you have endured was nothing to do with you because if you let yourself believe this then life will become much harder. Why? Because in this knowing you will have to take responsibility of what you have become. This teaching shows you that your frailty and need for growth brought you here, because this earth holds a unique purpose for you. Your life is a privileged state but the hardship of life has made you succumb to indifference. Rest when you need to, give yourself what you need to get through, and don't forget to wake from your sleep.

12.

To know what drives you is a fundamental question to living.

To know what drives you is a fundamental question to living. In modern life enormous pressure is created when you believe you must achieve externally and follow another's wish above your own. Searching for self-gain can never really give you what you need. To completely free the self is to know what is in you and live from this. Aligning to the hallowed presence is the knowing that life is a co-creative process, and that you do not own or control anything. Creating with honour is to live for the highest good of all. This place knows no owner-ship and so leads to the highest potential.

GUIDANCE   Why do you do the things you do? This may seem an obvious question but this will help you understand what drives you. This is not about creating an answer you want to hear yourself say but answer this in a true way. To learn about what you are is to awaken this conscious knowing. You may find what is driving you may not be what you thought. Accepting yourself is of great service to you, to not compare with what you feel you want others to see in you but what you are. If you have the wish to change any aspect of yourself that does not feel true to you then you must see what lies heavy in the heart.

13.

In your true state, life is lived from a vital and real source
dependant on nothing.

It is a constant challenge to fight against the collective disorder. In life the strengthening of the true self is the higher fight. You must begin to dream consciously, to awaken from your sleep and to see that you are the master of reality. What you think, feel and do matters in creating the reality you live in. In your true state, life is lived from a vital and real source dependant on nothing. This dream starts within and is in your hands. The highest power overcomes all discord and this truth is witnessed through inner knowing. You become blind to this when you are unable to see what feels too bright to hold. To live in light you must free yourself from what limits you. To support and nurture this call allows for empowerment to be.

GUIDANCE   In a world that is penetrated with fear, you are shown that you need to be dependant. It is often difficult to understand that the more you can stand apart and take responsibility, the more you take care of those around you. Be careful of the conditioning that brings to you a culture of disempowerment. Many people exist in discord and cannot always accept these truths. Each one of us must live truth independently and learn how to share our love from it. Instead people search for love externally and believe that this brings fulfilment. Love is the celebration of light and this is not forced into being.

Summary of Teachings

1. Purpose lies in the maturity of your light, for this is the pride of your existence where you integrate the higher self into life.

2. With self-knowledge and sensitivity belief is strong, where you break the ties from suffering and corruption.

3. By escaping into the external reality, you lose power.

4. You have not been given an impossible task, for you have evolved to this point and possess all you need to face the fears inside of you.

5. The Holy lives as the highest source of being and your potential lies in the realisation of it.

6. It's important to support each other and not condemn the natural process of healing.

7. When you cannot accept yourself then dissatisfaction in your external life continues.

8. You will experience resistance, within, and also through the collective consciousness.

9. The cream of life, the fullness of being, comes from emersion in your inner world, and following that which is true to you.

10. Your life force seeks joy and beauty effortlessly, for her creation is the essence of all impulses.

11. You chose this reality; you chose the earth beyond all other realities for realisation and to then go beyond this.

12. To know what drives you is a fundamental question to living.

13. In your true state, life is lived from a vital and real source dependant on nothing.

YOUR DESTINY IS IN YOUR HANDS

UNDERSTAND
with self-belief you steer destiny

LEARN
how surrendering within is the expansion
of you

BELIEVE
that wisdom lies in you

1.

The higher wish is to create out of power from within and to drive this dream.

In the true self you reside with higher powers that show you a clear road ahead. You have the ability to know all that you are, for you are the keeper of yourself. The higher wish is to create out of power from within and to drive this dream. Pain is a teacher, the holder of truth and all that is real. To move past pain is to open to what you feel, the doubts, struggle and fears, for only in the seeing of what you are, can you truly know what lies beyond. Pain heightens and prepares you by shifting you into a sensitive state. Without this you remain stuck in lower vibrations that cannot access the truth of pain. The coldness in life makes you forget sensitivity and so pain acts as the doorway back to the true sense of self.

GUIDANCE   You look to be validated by another so that you can be what you want. This longing is the wound in life that has bound us to searching for an authority outside the self. Your belief matters beyond all else, for when others walk away from you, you are faced with loneliness and so yearn to escape facing yourself. To feel the depths of you, brings up what you have suppressed for a long time, and opening feels overwhelming. This can be strong but it does not force you or subject you to anything that you cannot deal with. When you feel the path is too strong, seek guidance with this higher intention.

2.

To bring back yourself to light means a new training must come.

The shadows create corruption and all that is Holy becomes hidden. In forgetting who you are, you become a foreigner to yourself. To be free of discord is to breathe happiness. To bring yourself to light means a new training must come. To steer destiny is to follow what is authentic in you. Through belief you create the world you wish for and in turn manifest the future you desire from a true place within. When life is lived out of a true state of being, you shine. In this freeing you create from the Holy within. Living a full life is to find out who you are and what makes you. To breathe your way is the calling for the true self to emerge.

GUIDANCE   You come for healing because you want change, to remove blocks from happiness, to release pain, so that you become lighter, or to create harmony where there is discord. What cannot be determined is how this wish will come about. To bring about a new way of being means that you will change and what you have always known you cannot hold on to. Because you have held on you now have pain. To be on board this higher task you must be prepared to give it time and energy. You cannot expect that taking a little time out to fix you will bring change. You may feel momentarily better, but how you carry yourself afterwards is of greater benefit to you. What you awaken within needs you to tend to it, just like a newly planted seed. If you leave it and take the mind else-where, soon that shoot will be smothered by its environment and disappear. Change comes when your attention is a consist-ent companion.

3.

Oneness is when every part of the fragmented self has been inte-grated, where you are connected to the source of the creative self and where inner knowing meets your every need.

Your higher unfolding cannot be controlled or you become lost to further shadows. The brightness of light cannot be contained or moulded for it is unbound and limitless. In the oneness of being you are free from corruption and complete, for this is your natural state. Oneness is when every part of the fragmented self has been integrated, where you are connect-ed to the source of the creative self and where inner knowing meets your every need. Here, you do not wish for self gain but for the greater good of all. Aligned to the inner fire you are untethered and limitless. What ties you down is released. From this is the transformation to the higher potential. All that feels restrictive within is the opportunity for further belief to be realised. To live in endless suffering is not the higher truth but has come to awaken your power and to surrender to your light.

GUIDANCE   You know when there is fragmentation in you because you still search, feel the pain of discord and hold on to your desires. To find help to inner knowing is part of this path of opening. You become lost in the worry of how to start and what to do, becoming overwhelmed with the choices you need to make. This is why reaching to those who know this path reassures you and helps you to find relief that you are doing the best you can in this moment. When you feel lost in knowing which path to take, then don't be afraid to do nothing. The power of daily prayer is enough to bring you closer to this wish. Remind yourself that you are not alone and that the whole of creation beckons you forward to realise yourself. Sometimes just the asking is enough.

4.

Awakening comes from surrendering, not holding on to all that you think you are but embracing what you are.

When you lose the connection to inner truth you become filled with shadows. In facing fear you can believe again. To steer destiny is to catch yourself from the fall, to take responsibility of who you are and what you are becoming. Out of showing brings the realisation of what you want. When life is lived out of fear then what waits to be realised is freedom from it. Awakening comes from surrendering, not holding on to all that you think you are but embracing what you are. To live from an empowered state you must be honest to what you carry. Without letting go you remain restricted and limit expression. From the loss of your truth you forget how to believe.

GUIDANCE   You find yourself chasing the dream of what you think you should be, because of the need to control. Out of fear that lies within, you will force outcomes from the tight grip that you have of the image of yourself. The stronger you hold on, the more aggressive you will become in striving to what you believe must be. We hold on so much because the grief in the heart feels too much to bear. Understand that the intelligence in you is able to steer the way. It may not feel like you have what it takes to break this pattern, but you do. Yes it will take perseverance, and you may need help and support through it, but when you do it enough times you will get familiar and relief will come.

5.

When you steer destiny, the light in life becomes vast for that which is lived is your shining.

From direct experience of seeing yourself in all your colours, you become free, and this allows you to move past the illusion of pain. Living from inner truth you don't fear your growth but retain integrity of what you are becoming. No one can give you sovereignty. To be the authority of yourself must come from you. To see all parts of you is to go beyond discord and this is the awakening of light. The higher purpose is to create from the inner fire. This is when living is known in its higher state. To be the creator of life comes from witnessing the core of who you are. This comes from the conscious choice to surrender and accept yourself. Here can the destiny of you be felt. When you steer destiny, the light in life becomes vast for that which is lived is your shining. There is the potential in you to bring the Holy from pain and to forgive yourself. In fear you resist light. By going within, is the potential to go higher.

GUIDANCE   Listen to how the different aspects of yourself respond to external stimuli. This is learning about your physical body, emotional body, mental body or energy body. To bring sensitivity back to this level, you need to spend time with your inner reality. You can do this as a meditation, but not one that comes from force or is controlled. Relax into yourself, close your eyes and start to watch all the sensations that come up for you. When you spend time in the inner world something starts to change. Do nothing but watch the movement of you. Just like getting to know a stranger, you have to meet up quite a few times before you both start to relax and tune in to each other. If this is all you do to get to know the inner reality, you will see that something extraordinary happens to how you relate to the world around you. You can only know this when you try it. After you have done this for approximately fifteen minutes then start to interact with the world and notice what changes for you.

6.

The sadness of life comes when you become lost and empty within, for you lose trust in your ability to carry yourself.

Grief within is the evidence of unresolved pain. Having the courage to see through the shadows you heal. You struggle to do this for endless distractions pull you away from the prospect of seeing pain. From the window of pain in the heart is the potential to free into light. To lead is to bring about inner knowing. To bear the pain of the shadow frees you and removes you from the trap of time. Finding meaning from pain is the elevation to light. Belief comes out of feeling what is real to you. The sadness of life comes when you become lost and empty within, for you lose trust in your ability to carry yourself. When life becomes hard then you must bring yourself out of fear. When you are bereft of light, then inner truth is forgotten and you are bound in pain. To steer destiny is to find self-belief.

GUIDANCE   This reality is like an endless cycle. You only feel lost because you are unfamiliar with what lies inside of you. If you stay unfamiliar to yourself you believe that there is nothing there but the pain of instability. You presume this because you have no other proof other than the fear of yourself. In joining you meet who you are, you are not lost or empty only if you remain searching outside for stability. Your internal culture is what you believe. This is why it becomes valuable for you to explore the inner world because you must prove to yourself what you come with. All proving externally cannot bring light but an endless search to find what is real for you.

7.

Opening to the wish of the heart helps steer destiny and brings the power that lies within you.

To awaken power comes from taking away the restrictions that hold you back from the inner fire. What stops you is you become indifferent and allow others to lead you. Opening to the wish of the heart helps steer destiny and brings the power that lies within you. The true way is realised by living what you are in each moment, only then do you deliver light. Be aware of your choices and the intention of why you do the things you do. To understand who you are grows self-belief. The higher wish is to show and bring that which is your power to full manifest. To deliver out of what is true in the self is to come to what is real and what is Holy in the self.

GUIDANCE How to bring about self-governance is of significance. Life lived through the heart force takes you higher even if it brings you discomfort. Life becomes sterile when you keep only in the known. The heart is like a young child, curious, open and feeling the world through being, rather than from thought. You fear the heart because if it were to be free, you would not be able to logically understand it. You do not become mindless when you free the heart but you are held in the mystery of life, this is inner knowing rather than the knowing through the mind. Without this opening you bring about reality through the filters created to preserve yourself. To live this way reinforces a reality of separation, loneliness and isolation.

8.

To unlock life's mysteries with the mind alone gives you the wrong key, for what comes out of logic seeks to control from a limited place.

Direct perception of your response to life becomes clouded by the narrow vision of predetermined outcomes. To discern what is real from what is not becomes a struggle. From a place of fear and attachment you are not free to wonder and explore. Direct perception is reached from an open heart, untethered and uncontrolled. To unlock life's mysteries with the mind alone gives you the wrong key, for what comes out of logic seeks to control from a limited place. Wisdom cannot be derived from here. You must turn within to find out what you are looking for. To make this step you cannot avoid facing the shadow self. Without constraints on the heart you touch life sensitively and then there lies space for the expression of higher impulses.

GUIDANCE   When I work with someone who functions strongly from their mind, I see the powerful impact that it has in unbalancing the rest of their being. Their energy gravitates to the head and they effectively become top heavy. Little energy will flow in their legs and feet, resulting in poor circulation, and there is a disconnect to the earth. Without energy freely moving within, the person feels ungrounded, and can experience feeling unsafe or unstable in their selves. This in turn affects their feeling realm; they can be anxious, highly mistrusting and stressed. Helping the flow of energy to return throughout the body allows them to remember they are connected. In turn feeling safe and relaxed can return the energy flow for them to feel balanced again. The more someone is in their head, the more they seek to control.

9.

Wisdom is the integral part of being, for it is that which brings
reasoning and understanding to the way you are.

Pain exists to force you to question disharmony in being.
Managing yourself delivers you free from discord and drives
what you believe in. There is no rule book to life, how you do
this is up to you and you must do it your way. You drive yourself from the wisdom in you. What is life-giving is formed from
the creative force within. When aligned to this you create for
the highest good. When this is free within you then you live
the limitless aspect of you. When there is the awakening from
the higher self then there is wisdom. Wisdom is an integral
part of your being, for it is that which brings reasoning and
understanding to the way you are. To trust is to have wisdom
retrieved in you.

GUIDANCE   The power of understanding helps create you
and is paramount in healing. In the face of feeling lost in the
dark, or directionless, then you can understand what brought
you to this point, and this changes everything. In the moment
that something makes sense, light illuminates. Imagine then
something that you have run away from for so long is made
clear to you, why it happened to you, what it's teaching you
and how you can move on from it. All these aspects of healing
release you, and free energy for the higher purpose.

10.

By surpassing all borders in yourself and returning to the oneness experience you surrender in faith.

From your sovereignty there is no need to attach to another, for you know that you are free and so are others if they choose it. By surpassing all borders in yourself and returning to the oneness experience you surrender in faith. Without control you become conscious of what is unfolding in you and this accelerates your awakening. All that exists from the known cannot be of help, for true life functions in a new and vital way. What we try to fix, inhibits seeing. In every layer of being truth can be revealed. This is the flowering of the soul where the loving heart is in full bloom.

GUIDANCE   Faith is peace and in peace you have faith. Inner knowing strengthens the faith you have within. All the fighting in life, the aggression and torment exists because of the loss of faith. There is no replacement for this externally that provides the consistent knowing that you are one with light. Know that all that limits you, limits your faith. Freedom has nothing to do with success, material or psychological gain but is related to the ties that tether you from being in a true state of love. Potential is in truth and this sets you free. What remains to help you to rise higher comes from the natural state of being from within.

11.

At this time, developing your will power is the most prominent characteristic to grow.

The encouragement to follow another and be led comes from corruption. When you feel you must hold on to the external reality then you fall to the shadows and live out of self-preservation. This reality is of the most serious nature as it alters the ability to remain true to yourself and breeds further fear. To strive for safety and comfort outside the self is a false path to knowing inner truth. At this time, developing your will power is the most prominent characteristic to grow. You have the choice to develop this consciously or remain indifferent to it. The goal is the integration of the higher self and to manifest your will on earth. To live the inner fire within the physical realm is the gift of life.

GUIDANCE   Creating a strong will is the source of creating reality. With awareness, what you see within is what is real to you. You have dulled sensitivity potentially over life times, and now have become distant from your true voice, therefore don't forget that it can take a long time to regain this sense. Practice asking yourself when you come to the end of the day what was meaningful for you today. What touched you and brought you to the heart? You will find that what you see is what matters to you, and should not be ignored. Also notice if there was anything that you were trying to avoid seeing, an uncomfortable situation or feeling? Again this is showing you to not ignore this either. Belief in yourself comes from seeing what is real for you, the light and darker shades.

12.

You stop growing your potential and settle for what you are shown.

You stop growing your potential and settle for what you are shown. Instead you become lost to karma, unconsciously living out the price of past discord. To break out of this cycle, inner truth must be wished for in order for the breath of you to return. You become lost in grief and fear the way of empowerment. To allow the wisdom of you to lead you must gain trust in the inner world again. Surety comes when delivering out of the self. Here lies freedom and the belief in a higher potential.

GUIDANCE   It can seem the most baffling concept that you may want to hold yourself back from being empowered. The reason is very simple, when you live with discord and then grow light then this light will enhance the strength of your shadow also. Why? This is the creative balancing process of life, it shows us that when you move towards the higher potential then all that does not serve you must come to the surface and be released. This is crucial for the preparation of holding a higher light within. Empowerment is exactly that, it is powerful and you must be ready to manage this light. You are given all the circumstances you need to prepare yourself, you cannot side step them to get to light any quicker, as they are pivotal for your highest good.

13.

Empowerment comes when you are complete within.

Living in balance is to learn how to manage your life. Life is not lived for another but from self-belief, for here is the natural state of being. When you listen to yourself then you are carried by the sustaining life force within you. You are seeking how to live, to remember the light within and to continue to ask for your way. In the fall you hide from pain and become separated from what is Holy and what is not. You lose yourself in external wanting and search outside of you to find peace. Opening to what you feel within brings about the true realisation of the limitless self. When you follow what you are to where you need to go then you will come to the higher dream. Empowerment comes when you are complete within.

GUIDANCE   Empowerment brings you to your light and sets you free from discord. When you settle for something not because you believe in it but for other reasons this is what you show life. Your energy does not move from your light, but a diluted version of it, and so the world believes this is you, and brings what meets you on this vibrational level. You get used to this frequency and changing it feels too much effort. When you live making choices from what you believe, where your heart is aligned with your higher sensitivity, this raises your energy to one that is full of life and empowered. In turn this is how the world reads you, and again will bring to you what matches your energy. To steer your destiny with light is be conscious of what you believe in, and to create your life from it.

Summary of Teachings

1. The higher wish is to create out of power from within and to drive this dream.

2. To bring yourself to light means a new training must come.

3. Oneness is when every part of the fragmented self has been integrated, where you are connected to the source of the creative self and where inner knowing meets your every need.

4. Awakening comes from surrendering, not holding on to all that you think you are, but embracing what you are.

5. When you steer destiny, the light in life becomes vast, for that which is lived is your shining.

6. The sadness of life comes when you become lost and empty within, for you lose trust in your ability to carry yourself.

7. Opening to the wish of the heart, helps steer destiny and brings the power that lies within you.

8. To unlock life's mysteries with the mind alone gives you the wrong key, for what comes out of logic seeks to control from a limited place.

9. Wisdom is the integral part of being, for it is that which brings reasoning and understanding to the way you are.

10. By surpassing all borders in yourself and returning to the oneness experience you surrender in faith.

11. At this time, developing your will power is the most prominent characteristic to grow.

12. You stop growing your potential and settle for what you are shown.

13. Empowerment comes when you are complete within.

No One Else Can Get Your Light But You

UNDERSTAND
that pain is a bridge to the creative force
within you

LEARN
how you live your fire by untethering the
ties that hold you back

BELIEVE
that living with pain is not your true state
of being

1.

Blindly taking in constructs created by others takes you away from your true sense of purpose, for that can only come from following yourself.

In the struggle for power, how you see others becomes significant. If you cannot find stability within, you have to seek it from someone else and so this becomes the focus. The sentiment of needing another to achieve power fills life with discord energy. Corruption is born from self-preservation. Blindly taking in constructs created by others takes you away from your true sense of purpose, for that can only come from following yourself. Instead of self-belief, doubt and fear is bred. To rely on inner truth illuminates the path ahead. You are learning not to fight but to surrender to yourself. Through the acceptance of pain you can start to learn the higher teachings of why pain has come, and what you need to learn from it.

GUIDANCE   You are being shown how to do things throughout all your life. To blindly follow means to accept what someone gives you without knowing how you feel about it. This can happen instantaneously to not 'see' yourself, but to accept and do what you are shown. This teaching shows you to be aware of the impression that this exchange has on you. When you negate your response, you lose the opportunity to see if what you are being shown resonates in a true way for you. How do you know this? You do this by being aware of the impulses within you and how you respond to them. Through this information you can choose to integrate it as part of your reality or not. This builds inner sensitivity, and aligns you to what is real for you.

2.

To remain on the surface of you brings powerlessness, for you give attention to others more than you are conscious of.

When you live from the surface of yourself you take life at face value. Without going deeper into your being, the essence of your truth is kept away. From the challenge of the fall is the calling to face self-corruption and fear within you. Life cannot come to balance without this level of engagement. The creative force which is driving life becomes tainted with fear from the collective consciousness. To remain on the surface of you brings powerlessness, for you give attention to others more than you are conscious of.

GUIDANCE   Your power comes by knowing yourself in a deeper and meaningful way. The surface self is the part of you that merely functions and is the image of you that you try and uphold to others. To go deeper is to let go of the constraints of what you think you should be, to look at what you are and the experience of you. Many people function at this level, where the heart remains hidden and you act out of the false self to fit in. To breathe life into the soul is to allow yourself to move past the surface and turn attention inwards. This must be practiced for you have developed a strong habit to looking outside of you and so even more effort is needed to turn inwards.

3.

When you face pain, it is inevitable that you will question your path in life.

Lost in the race of proving yourself to others creates suffering. Suffering comes from the seeds of poverty within. Out of truth can this reality be changed. When you face pain, it is inevitable that you will question your path in life. Releasing the discord that lies behind pain reveals the substance of what you are and what you come with. Without discord you cannot know how you came to be the way you are. With every release comes this seeing, this is truth where self-belief is generated. Giving attention to a reality that stems from discord, the cycle of pain and pleasure becomes never ending. Only in the self can belief return and this brings liberation from discord. In the journey to oneness, you integrate all parts of the fragmented self and understand the true path created for you. Your fall gives the potential to overcome fear.

GUIDANCE   Introspection is part of spiritual development. To make conscious that which is unconscious is of service to you and your future. Waking up from a sleep state is to come out of the darkness, and see yourself for what you really are. Humility comes when you see the sensitivity of being in relationship to life. Going within you meet the curiosity of your nature, where you cannot help but want to understand more. With each inner enquiry comes the fertile terrain where wisdom lies. What you hold within is light, and this waits for you to explore yourself. In opening you create space to know and understand the direction that you are heading in.

4.

*To have inner knowing, is to challenge what feels restricted
internally, and learn how it was created.*

Through the continuous cycle of life and death is the
chance to retrieve power. You are propelled to understand
yourself and to awaken from the sleep state of powerlessness.
The processes of life's cycles are karmic and are mirrors that
reflect how tethered the true self has become. The sentiment
of higher love comes to know itself through life. To have love
manifest from higher living you must awaken from the fall.
Everything that moves within you, thoughts and feelings are
creating your reality. When you deviate from inner knowing
you will turn outwards to gain it. But this is conditional and
transitory, always based on the circumstances and people
outside of you. Pulling away from the inner world creates a
life with division. To have inner knowing, is to challenge what
feels restricted internally, and learn how it was created. The
inner life has the potential to provide you with everything
you need to live a sustainable, fulfilling and peaceful life. The
calling which was originally to light is now answering to fear
instead. When fear becomes eradicated from being, then all
that remains is love. Grief comes from the loss of the essence
of the true self. Beyond life and death is truth, this is the praising of life.

GUIDANCE   Inner restrictions comes in so many ways,
through the physical, you may experience tensions, stiffness,
disease, pain or sickness. The emotional, you feel anxiety, grief,
anger, fear, shock or hate. The mental disharmony creates

paranoia, worry, shame, controlling thoughts or hallucinations. The energetic aspect of you becomes dull, lifeless, heavy, fragmented, attacked or disconnected. These are only some of the distortions of being when we become restricted. We run away from all this discord in the fear that we will be overwhelmed by suffering. To accept what you carry must come slowly but what is often true is that you try to escape from the discomfort in you. In a paced way life is asking you to start this journey.

5.

You cannot know the tenderness of care if you only seek to build stability outside of yourself.

When insecurity is created from fear, care becomes careless. You cannot know the tenderness of care if you only seek to build stability outside of yourself. True care shows itself when it rises from pain, when you are forced to see the fragility of being. Without seeing your vulnerability you believe that you are secure, but this is a false security if it merely comes from external sources. Seeing from the heart you know care. Care derives from the heart force. Hearing the higher call comes from a place where there is no fear and where the power of the inner path reigns. Self-belief and conviction comes from truth. You cannot be lost when this power is followed. Blindly following another to find your way creates corruption. From direct experience can the outer reality be lived in a meaningful way.

GUIDANCE   You will live with the tension of anticipation when you ask for care to be externally brought to you and not through you. You can outwardly do caring tasks, but still not know care within you. We have become good at fooling ourselves that our lives are created with care, we fight in the name of it and yet this is not care. What lies in the tenderness of being cannot be given to you but experienced in you. You can see this in your worries and tension that you carry, when you don't know if something you really want externally will come or not. You become lost in this distraction, and what is care inside of you becomes placed to the side. To know the tenderness of the inner nature is to know care.

6.

The reality of fear and suffering is willingly accepted as a belief and that it cannot exist in any other way.

Trust within can feel an impossible task to retrieve. To expand the true self is to have courage to turn inwards and catch yourself from the fall. Understanding how pain is created can untangle you from it and set you free. The reality of fear and suffering is willingly accepted as a belief and that it cannot exist in any other way. Willingness to face personal struggle and surrender to it, opens you to the higher potential. The true self is cheated in life and terror becomes a directing force. Fragmentation creates a powerful struggle where the higher aspect of you is limited. What may seem empty within you is concealing the force of the creative fire. You live the inner fire when you are free from the ties that hold you back.

GUIDANCE   To consider that the potential of you is free from suffering reconnects you with remembering your origins.

Even if it feels a far removed reality you are part of a higher intelligence of knowing. To awaken supreme consciousness in the weave of life is to start by knowing that you are an important part of its fruition. We are living in a time where the healing process is happening much quicker and as time passes this will be accelerated. To see this is a great blessing for human evolution. To bring the higher potential that this lends itself to, it must be made conscious and active in you. You cannot side step your involvement in creating reality. To face pain has never been so supported and driven as it is now. Taking the reins of yourself is taking responsibility and playing your part in it.

7.

To create change, you are asked to believe in your truth and to know this.

Peace cannot be acquired from outside of you. What is achieved from the inner path is the deliverance of the higher calling. Your greater potential manifests when you are unlimited and free from inner borders. Turning inwards many are frightened to see their personal conflict. Doubt follows fear. You hesitate when you try to hold on to external security, even though it is not your truth it is all you have known. To create change, you are asked to believe in your truth and to know this. When life is lived from the surface then true understanding cannot be reached. What brings meaning is to step into the unknown of you and reveal the deeper feelings within. The real aspect of you is fearless, where all doubts are answered.

GUIDANCE   An invincible power of will is created when you follow light within. Life wants you to be the greatest aspect of you. This is forgotten when those around you also live from a false sense of self. Now to shine is a rarity. Love is what you are striving for. Empowerment needs courage of will. Believe that the path of truth frees not just yourself but all those around you. You have the potential to change the reality you live. You do not leave anyone behind but offer with love the realisation of being and this will naturally influence others to light.

8.

When aligned to inner truth, the external life has the means to create lasting fulfilment.

No one can get your light but you, this is truth. Understanding inner life over outer pursuits can fear be overcome. In the fear of death is the trap of time, where your present life is believed to be all. When aligned to inner truth, the external life has the means to create lasting fulfilment. Clarity in life comes from the true source within. When you fear you turn outwards to get your needs met. Following others to lead the way promotes even further fear. It is up to you to remember the wish of this higher expression. Power is created out of self-belief. What comes from discord in the world makes us believe that we are strangers in life. In grief is a hidden fear, where we become distracted from imagining what we have lost. Through our tears is the mourning for the true self to become and the loss of it. Grief in life is the reminder of the separation from the oneness state. To understand this lament can your higher potential be realised.

GUIDANCE   You are not being shown that external life has no value for this is not the teaching. Inner life is the foundation of you and creates the outer life. If the foundation of you is disconnected, fragmented and unstable, you create this in the external reality. Your expression in the world is the celebration of you. You have not been designed to suffer in some hardship in life, but here lies a higher teaching for you. Being in touch with the fountain of light that resides in you is when you live the life you were created for. Love, happiness and peace can come effortlessly. The dream of this must be awakened in you to live it.

9.

The experience of pain has forced you to shut off from feeling and become lost to hardened thoughts.

Explaining the mystery of life through logic alone cannot express the true sentiments that are felt within. Understanding life through the feeling realm is the connection to a higher state of being. The experience of pain has forced you to shut off from feeling and become lost to hardened thoughts. Belief is realised when pain is faced and where you retrieve the power that you have lost. It is without a doubt a challenging journey to realise yourself through pain. This brings the courage you need. Absolute belief is a choice to move towards. If belief is obtained outside of you then it is for the pursuit of achieving. Pain is the doorway to remembering the wonder of being. With release, pain is the bridge to the creative force of life where you experience freedom and the abundance in nature.

GUIDANCE   The healthy functioning of the heart is no more valuable than the healthy functioning of the mind. This teaching is not questioning whether the mind powers are better or worse than the heart. We are looking at the distorted effects that inner disharmony creates on the nature of human expression. The heart, when open, is able to inform the power of the mind in the creating process. Each part is essential for higher development. When the heart is closed you block the path to moving freely towards the higher expression. Valuable information that is true to the essence of you cannot reach the mind when the heart is not open. You will not create from what feels true for you, but instead from information you gain from your external reality. To create this way you experience a small part of the potential and experience of yourself.

10.

Exploring the inner world reflects how creation on earth is being expressed in only a fraction of its potential.

The glow of internal power is magnificent. Exploring the inner world reflects how creation on earth is being expressed in only a fraction of its potential. When you feel this potential in you, power of belief grows. To carve the path firmly towards this reality, you must release the tie to the past and free from holding on to the future. This cannot be achieved by knowledge alone. Life for many becomes a feared place, where external forces seem greater in their dominance over you. To figure your own breath, you must steadily and slowly release that which is created through grief.

GUIDANCE   Many know this fact but have little under-standing of what moves them closer to this higher potential. These teachings offer guidance on this path and give the orien-tation you need to believe in yourself. You can lose hope, the will to fight and become lost to despair. Someone can give you the idea of hope, strength and will but cannot do it for you. To find relief in a world of pressure is very important and when you are ready you will rise again. The light in you burns regardless of you seeing it, what waits is following your way to living this dream.

11.

You may conceive the promise of light through the outer reality,
but it lies within you to be found.

It has been long forgotten what the real fight is. Your truest expression is greatly challenged at this time. To live into the higher self does not seek to conquer life but to know itself. In remembering, that only you can get your light, is the promise of the higher potential. There is the belief that empowerment is achieved outside of you. This is transitory compared to the true power that lies within. Yearning to achieve outside of you causes you to drift towards corruption, where indifference leads to powerlessness. Fear has no place in the greatness of you. Without belief through the heart you cannot receive light, for it comes from truth. You cannot cheat the true self, for as soon as you do suffering follows. This cannot be done for you or given to you by another as such sentiments must be driven by your hands alone. What is already present within is accessible for everyone. In forgetting the self you seek another to imagine truth. You may conceive the promise of light through the outer reality, but it lies within you to be found.

GUIDANCE There is great benefit to reading sacred texts, they act as channels to awaken the memory of your origins. Being studious alone cannot reach liberation. The experience of being is a felt sense. A powerful way to integrate what you read is to go slowly. Each time you read something stop every 3 to 4 sentences and notice its effect on you. Does it touch you, move you, make you feel something and if so what? When you allow things to touch you, this creates meaning. You have become used to taking in information quickly and this is counter-productive to creating a meaningful life that is of value to you. Without slowing down this process, and allowing yourself to meet the world, you experience only a small part of the depth in you.

12.

Moving away from living a heart centred life creates
fragmentation in you.

In the modern world it becomes a struggle to fulfil yourself. Moving away from living a heart centred life creates fragmentation. The consequence of this causes isolation, self-preservation and survival at any cost. Reaching freedom, you must awaken from the discord created and turn inwards to heal. Without the conscious movement to turning within, there lies the need to prove yourself in external pursuits. Over life times, inner truth has been compromised within the soul. This compromise has moved you far from the true sense of living. Light in yourself is dulled when sensitivity becomes overpowered. Here lies the collective despair to creating a different reality. In the return to accepting the sensitivity of what you feel can true clarity and self-belief be realised.

GUIDANCE   When you base the way you live from external sources alone, then this cannot be real for you. In the heart you know what exists as true, no matter what is true for someone else. Every person has a different path and you must follow yours to live light. Confusion, pain and suffering come from the discord created within. In discord you move away from what lies at the core of you. When discord is resolved within, then you will come back to clarity, direction and impulses. What is real for you starts in the heart.

13.

From higher consciousness you begin your chosen calling and karma no longer dictates what comes.

In the realisation of oneness, all that remains is love. Surrendering to yourself sets you free to live a boundless state where freedom waits. From higher consciousness you begin your chosen calling and karma no longer dictates what comes. If power is sought from external sources then it will be conditional where true love cannot flourish. From direct experience of all the shades of you can you come to the oneness state. In truth, you can see what you come for and know yourself. Understand that the inner realm is the vehicle for transformation. Empowerment of yourself comes from the brightness of you. You cannot blame another for the state of the world but accept your part in it.

GUIDANCE   To be free of karma is your true destiny. In one way or another life is constantly driving to get you there, no matter the mysterious lengths in which the path takes. To live without karma is to be free of discord. You will still feel life, but you are no longer distracted by the disharmony of pain. In light your purpose is made clear. Generalisation of what to expect or how this will feel is of no service to you. Your realisation and purpose cannot be dictated by anyone, and all manner of expectation is futile. The true mystery of creation cannot be ordered, patterned or deciphered. You cannot hold on to what you believe will come. The best you can do is live your truth, and allow others to do the same.

Summary of Teachings

1. Blindly taking in constructs created by others takes you away from your true sense of purpose, for that can only come from following yourself.

2. To remain on the surface of you brings powerlessness, for you give attention to others more than you are conscious of.

3. When you face pain, it is inevitable that you will question your path in life.

4. To have inner knowing, is to challenge what feels restricted internally, and to learn how it was created.

5. You cannot know the tenderness of care if you only seek to build stability outside of yourself.

6. The reality of fear and suffering is willingly accepted as a belief and that it cannot exist in any other way.

7. To create change, you are asked to believe in your truth and to know this.

8. When aligned to inner truth, the external life has the means to create lasting fulfilment.

9. The experience of pain has forced you to shut off from feeling and become lost to hardened thoughts.

10. Exploring the inner world reflects how creation on earth is being expressed in only a fraction of its potential.

11. You may conceive the promise of light through the outer reality, but it lies within you to be found.

12. Moving away from living a heart centred life creates fragmentation in you.

13. From higher consciousness you begin your chosen calling and karma no longer dictates what comes.

LIVE THE LIFE OF EMPOWERMENT

UNDERSTAND
with acceptance you live empowered

LEARN
that you have the power to forgive yourself

BELIEVE
from union with the creative life force, you come
to the sovereignty of being

1.

The potential to hear the call of your true voice, comes in the darkest hour.

What life is for, how to live it and why you exist is answered from within. From the separation of oneness you became disempowered. To return to wholeness and regain self-belief, healing for the soul must happen on all levels of being. Moving past the illusion of pain answers all your questions. Facing fear you come to the higher aspect of you and bring forth your truth. The potential to hear the call of your true voice, comes in the darkest hour. To trust is to know you can lead yourself and feel the freedom that lies within.

GUIDANCE We desperately want to make things feel tidy and presentable. On a large scale the human psyche fears darkness, and creates a reality that aggressively attacks and punishes its presence. From a place of peace, darkness is accepted, as is all of life's creation. To know this is a higher truth, for it is only when you accept inner darkness can you accept it in life. We betray this part of ourselves and so lose connection to the whole aspect of being. The effect of this weakens the soul, and so we break trust with our self. If you stigmatise something, you reinforce a reality of fear. This becomes the accepted illusion that you buy into. We sensationalise pain and demonise fear. Yes toxic energy has a different expression to light, but it remains as part of creation, also needing expression. When you are able to move past the constructs of good and bad, dark and light, then you can respond to life in a real way.

2.

Going beyond what is known to you, is key to unlocking your higher potential.

The stream of life that created the earth, knows the sovereignty of its creation. What lives from this truth, unfolds through the interconnectedness of all life. In the wheel of life, you are given the task to break free. The fight is not to each other but to face fear and to live your personal truth. With life times of self-corruption, powerlessness is generated to a great scale. To choose and direct life meaningfully in line with truth, becomes a difficult task. Instead there lies the shadow of indifference and apathy. You fall to rise again. In turning away from truth, is the search to return to it. Going beyond what is known to you, is key to unlocking your higher potential. You come into life for this purpose, to create the self whole again.

GUIDANCE   Freedom is just that, it belongs to a place that is not known logically. If you try to form it, this would not be freedom but would come from the mind that wishes to conclude and fixate. When you experience true freedom, the process of holding on is not a reality any more, for in oneness you are empowered. This is the path for higher evolution. You cannot truly speculate about the wisdom, interconnectedness and love that will express itself through you. Each one of us can access this truth, and live the light that we are. From an empowered state the potential of life is unlimited.

3.

You become conditioned from the collective discord, and so turn away from what makes you stand apart.

That which is sustainable comes from your inner fire. The tricks of life calls you to follow another to gain what you want. You become conditioned from the collective discord, and so turn away from what makes you stand apart. To break away from this illusion is the challenge. Though great things are accomplished externally, this is incomparable to what lies within. Only in the surrendering to what is inside of you, can you live empowered. You came into life, to free from pain and suffering and live your potential. In living, you can find truth. The answers to all that you wish for is found within. To live life from the inner way, brings you to your higher purpose.

GUIDANCE   We force our self to be or act a certain way. You are told to be caring and respect others. You are fed with many versions of what this looks like, and so try to force its expression, even when it does not feel real to you. This teaching does not tell you to abandon what is caring in life, but asks you to believe in a care that comes through the most authentic part of you. When you do this you live what is real, and not a second hand version. To realise this, you must trust yourself. Imagine when you may have lost trust in someone and have to rebuild it again. This requires you to go slower, you become more sensitive, and realise that you can't take anything for granted. This is also what you experience when you rebuild trust in yourself.

4.

Over and over again, has the experience of broken dreams caused despondency in you.

When there is control, life is stifled, oppressed and feared. Little space is created and the ability for connection in the world becomes a struggle. Feeling the touch of the world, you see what is truly there. Life becomes misguided and meaningless when you shut off feeling. Living from inner belief comes when you are integrated with the heart self. Without this, you sense yourself as separate and life becomes compartmentalised. Over and over again, has the experience of broken dreams caused despondency in you. Through lifetimes you grow, and you move closer towards clearing the way.

GUIDANCE   When we lose higher perspective, there is the danger of looking at the self with a narrow vision. Often from fear you compare yourself to others, feeling as if your life is worthless, or less than what you see others go through. Comparing life processes with another is futile. What brings relief is to know how past lives may have fed into the intensity of your process today. Often when people carry intense trauma or emotions, it is because this has been with them through life times. When the person is ready, whether in this life time or another, they will release this karmic tie. We are intricate and soulful beings, that come with many layers that still only few can see. Knowing that you have been travelling a long time with what you carry, helps you to see that the depth of you is vast and no other can compare to you. What lies in you is yours, what you have gone through is unique to you, no matter how different you look to another.

5.

*When you became separated from the higher path,
you lost power.*

All struggles that come into life, are from the loss of connection within. When you became separated from the higher path, you lost power. By turning to sensitivity within, struggle and oppression can be eliminated. To seek control has limited you, and so life is created from little meaning. Searching for meaning externally, can only take you so far. Seeing yourself without distortion, resistance or manipulation brings you to truth. To control is the distortion of you. You are empowered where there is no need for control, for all is accepted. That which opens the self fully, is found from the higher sensitivity within. Through the interconnectedness of yourself, you create the world you wish to live in.

GUIDANCE   The higher wish is to search for nothing, to know peace and love. When this occurs life vibrates on a powerful level. Knowing the potential of you, is the start to realising it. When you dream into life you create. This is not a dreaming that is full of control and aggression. Riding the creative stream of life, you can explore your greatness. Sensitivity is key to knowing your higher state. Opening the heart allows sensitivity to become more refined. Releasing pain, is part of the path that takes you higher, for it prepares you to carry more light as you expand. Without release, fear limits your growth. The wisdom of your unique healing journey, prepares you for your higher purpose.

6.

A power is birthed with every truth that is ignited within you.

The battle in the true self is for belief. In the fall you lose power and forget who you really are. A power is birthed with every truth that is ignited within you. Each time you take responsibility, you step closer to a greater power that lies within. Tapping into the creative flow of life, is where truth lies. To live what is real for you, is the task of life. Remembering this with perseverance, then care is truly lived in life. Hope is cast from self-belief, for you know how to deliver yourself to the dream of what you came for. Opening to vulnerability, you take the role as a researcher of truth. You become scared of your vulnerability and so try to hide what you are. You must let go of your expectations and insistence to mould your pain, and go with it. The higher place of being knows how to drive itself and trust its truth.

GUIDANCE   Belief comes when you listen to the truth of yourself. You forgot this, because you become complacent and apathetic to the inner world. From discord others can take advantage of your complacency. What for? It is hard to believe when you feel low, that another has anything to gain from you. But when belief is not strong within you, the will becomes weak, and this is when you succumb to following others easily. The preciousness of your life is a great treasure, whether you are struggling within or not. Those who truly wish for the highest good for you, will not ask you to follow them, but will seek to empower you.

7.

When you believe that you have the power to forgive yourself,
then you become liberated from suffering.

Freeing from the struggle to find the true self, is to know forgiveness. When you believe that you have the power to forgive yourself, then you become liberated from suffering. This level of surrender, is your empowered state. We create the path we lead, and through us alone can we return to light. What is real within, is to live in the true sovereignty of being. Through grief you realise the higher dream, and unlock the innate power within. You are given the opportunity to awaken in life and manifest all that you are. From the fear that exists in the world, you have a choice to support it or not. When mastering inner fear, you live the creative potential. When you choose to perpetuate the destruction of life, you encourage the sentiments of self-gain and the acquisition of external power. This place is torment to the soul. This reality exists because you believe in it. When you are able to challenge it's presence within, you can consciously transform your reality.

GUIDANCE   This illusion has shadowed the heart of man. The dream of the empowered state, is governed by what we believe in. We live in a new time, where truth can be the guiding force, and where fearing each other can be transformed to light. No longer do we need another to save us, for that which is the living light is present in all. The grace of God comes when you forgive yourself. You have to wander deep into your pain for this blessing, and find release from inner torment. When awakened, the gate to universal knowledge is opened. To not fear yourself, delivers you.

8.

To return to balance you must address imbalance.

The essence of the true self is not corrupt. It lies beyond all shadows and pain. Your being is complete, and its truth is beyond all suffering. This is the essence of the creative life force. To live without polarities means to walk the middle path. The middle path is perfect balance, to break the illusion of polarity, and create through the foundation of careful living. In the natural world, you can see how fragile the earth is when it is out of balance. Extreme conditions in nature heal through disease and even destruction, before it can return to balance and harmony again. This movement, to regain balance is also innate in all living beings. To return to balance you must address imbalance. Living carefully is the awareness of this fragile process, and supporting your natural flow towards harmony. The balancing process is a constant healing task, to understand and master. To ignore this natural flow creates further disease, corruption and pain. Lost in the rush of external life, you choose to distract yourself from this natural law. To resist discord creates the fight in life. To give attention to this unfolding brings realisation.

GUIDANCE   You are always changing, even if you feel you are not. Each moment you experience a different impulse and impression that is unique to you. What is often a myth about healing, is that you can find a miracle cure. Yes, each power retrieved is bringing you closer to completeness, but the journey is not over. I experience that people are desperate to gain this full stop. When you are untethered from karma and live free from suffering, then you begin to unfold the experience of your complete self. But nothing stops. We imagine that enlightenment and self-realisation comes with an end. What this teaching shows, is life is ever growing and touching you and the fullness of yourself continues to bring a higher light. The journey is not over. You are sentient, creative being with a powerful life force, that will want to eternally express itself.

9.

Being able to show who you are, makes the will of the heart stronger.

Grief remains in you as a reminder to answer the highest call. The call is to the deepest wish in the self, to realise forgiveness to the loss of oneness. In living you learn to be the master, and live through the core truth of you. To avoid fear is to avoid yourself. To live through the creative power is delivered by the self alone. Coming within achieves this; to wander in the inner realms in a careful way, liberates you. Where love is, then the creative life force brings it's unique expression. In life you can come to live the higher self and to find purpose. When this wish is allowed to express itself, then living is created out of truth. To create the self, is to become conscious and aware of all that you are, and that which drives you. Being able to show who you are, makes the will of the heart stronger. In showing can your creative light know forgiveness in the heart.

GUIDANCE   Every choice you make either gives you life or brings you down. To sit on the fence of life, is to not know what fulfils you. Your sensitivity is dulled, through all the choices you make that don't come from your truth. In life we come to know the vulnerability of our being, and to feel the pain of the heart. You can break the cycle of indifference right now, stop and feel how these words affect you, are you touched by them and if so how? Know that any response is perfect, there is no right or wrong, for this is your truth. To break a habit of indifference, you must create new pathways. When a choice comes your way, remember to choose the path that touches you, then you know you are creating from a meaningful place.

10.

We can help each other to become visible, and promote the sentient parts of the self.

We can help each other to become visible, and promote the sentient parts of the self. Your way of seeing is powerful. To live out of power, is to learn to seek the answers from within and surrender to that. Within you lies the Holy, where you are free. This is the higher dream wanting to be realised. All that remains significant to the true self, comes out of a higher sensitivity. All that touches the heart, is what remains your everlasting truth. Without this sensitivity you become lost to the world. In life is the opportunity to learn about the carefulness of living. To create through light, is what obtains it in the world.

GUIDANCE   To live with humility, is to treat others how you wish to be treated. Unconditional love becomes limited from the demanding pressure that is created in life. When you pause to know what lies in you, this allows another to feel your courage. Though our stories bring different strengths, our words of encouragement to each other are powerful. We cannot rescue each other, that is in our hands alone, and must be for the higher state of life to be realised. We are here together on the same journey. When you find yourself judging or criticising another, know that you burden yourself further. Bring the wish of peace to everyone, no matter the level of discord they come with, and this is the reality that you will nurture in yourself.

11.

Awakening from fear is not your highest potential, but is the stepping stone to living your supreme self.

What is worth carrying begins in the heart. This is how you believe. This awakens the path to the Holy. Awakening from fear is not your highest potential, but is the stepping stone to living your supreme self. That which you are learning to do, is to set your inner fire free. Without limitations placed within the heart, the path is made clear. Living with distortion, allows only for tokens of this potential to exist. The sentiments of the heart are powerful. Its resonance penetrates deep into the fabric of all life. When you consciously grow this awareness, trust is created and in turn raises you higher.

GUIDANCE   It may take us lifetimes to free ourselves from fear, but this is the greatest battle to win. What lies ahead of you, is your making, for without fear you cannot live your light. To have the burden of suffering lifted, is but a small part of what you have yet to create. With the millions of years of suffering that the world has come to know, it will one day fade as a distant memory. It will be replaced with the wonder of the creative fire, which lives to grow life with an incomprehensible light. For you to dream this vision, you must clear the path that restricts you from your light. Each one of us has responsibility in its creation. Helping each other to find empowerment realises this dream for all.

12.

All that is not suppressed, bound or limited is the true self.

Love is let in when you allow the power of the creative force to lead you, and trust its guidance. All that is not suppressed, bound or limited is the true self. You need no other than this, to realise the higher potential. What lies in the oneness of being is to free into the higher self. Here the light of creation is found. When you become visible to the world, then love comes in. To witness your vulnerability, shows that you are open. From vulnerability you come to peace in the heart, where creating in life comes from truth. Love is, when you surrender to what lies in the heart, and the acceptance of all that you are. In self-realisation, you find freedom and empowerment.

GUIDANCE   To not forget to fill life with what uplifts you, is of great service to you. You are not responsible for what comes towards you, but what comes through you and is created from you. Learn how to bring life giving impulses into daily life. Do it in a way that feels like you and not in the way that others want you to. These teachings show you that there can be no short cuts, or miracle cures in reaching your light. Nurture strength in you, bring about the sentiments that lift you and this creates the world you wish to live in. What you love to see, touch and do, feeds you. To fill life with these sentiments, grows your light.

13.

Supreme consciousness is, when the heart and will are aligned to the higher self, and your fire is ignited.

Supreme consciousness is, when the heart and will are aligned to the higher self, and your fire is ignited. To be at one with the creative life force, is to be fearless and this is love. There lies no separation, for the self is this force. The Holy lives within you and without, in all of existence. When this matrimony awakens, there can only be eternal peace. The dream is to come into the essence of love. From the consistent perseverance of facing fear, can the heart be set free, to creating its unlimited truth. In the return to oneness, do you detach from the struggle of the external fight. The doorway to bliss lies within. True inner knowing is what guides you and the highest sacred truth waits. Merging with the Holy, comes when their lies no separation in the self. To steer destiny, is to find realness and bring that which is true in you alive. That which is light, lies beyond all suffering, for it has always known this calling and always will.

GUIDANCE   Like a flower, there are many layers in you that wish to unfold before you come to full bloom. It is not about the length of the journey or the time it takes, this is a path that has no rules. Decide to become and you will, how you will get there is yet to be known. Co-creation is the realisation that light is part of a greater force that flows in all matter. There is no value, no hierarchy or ultimate destination. Opening follows no predetermined path. You can remember your origins, for you know yourself. You are light, which means that which has been, will be again.

What has been will be again.

Summary of Teachings

1. The potential to hear the call of your true voice, comes in the darkest hour.

2. Going beyond what is known to you, is key to unlocking your higher potential.

3. You become conditioned from the collective discord, and so turn away from what makes you stand apart.

4. Over and over again, has the experience of broken dreams caused despondency in you.

5. When you became separated from the higher path, you lost power

6. A power is birthed with every truth that is ignited within you.

7. When you believe that you have the power to forgive yourself, then you become liberated from suffering.

8. To return to balance you must address imbalance.

9. Being able to show who you are makes, the will of the heart stronger.

10. We can help each other to become visible, and promote the sentient parts of the self.

11. Awakening from fear is not your highest potential, but is the stepping stone to living your supreme self.

12. All that is not suppressed, bound or limited is the true self.

13. Supreme consciousness is, when the heart and will are aligned to the higher self, and your fire is ignited.

When there is a prayer in each one's heart,

life will free itself and open to the splendour of its greatness.

Beyond all time will life become and

a great peace will fall on the earth.

Blessed be all beings. In the name of the Holy One

within each of us is given this truth.

Glossary

ACCEPTANCE   Being without resistance. When receiving, you are receptive and open within.

ANTI-BEING   That which goes against the nature of the true self and originates from a limited and restricted expression.

BELIEF   The guiding principle that is the foundation of all that you are. Conviction from the teachings of your truth.

CALLING   A deep longing that comes through the heart and is aligned to a higher state of being.

CO-CREATION   Living interconnected from the impulses inside and outside of you. Not against or separate to the creative life force but one with it.

COURAGE   Offering yourself in the face of adversity without necessarily knowing what is to come.

CORRUPTION   The counter force that goes against your innate truth of being. It creates hardship and discord.

CREATIVE LIFE FORCE   The movement of energy that flows within and connects all matter. The communion of life and is the essence of love.

DARK   The shadow of light. It came to be from the separation of the oneness state.

DISCORD   Fragmented and blocked energy.

EMPOWERMENT   Realisation and completion of the oneness state.

INNER FIRE   The alignment of the heart, will and higher self. The essence of sovereignty.

FORGIVENESS   To unburden from suffering. The experience of acceptance, release and relief.

FRAGMENTATION   Division created within the soul from the corruption of one's true state.

GRIEF   The experience of loss and sorrow.

HEART   The super-sensitive channel of the soul.

HIGHER SELF   The expansive state of your true being. The origin of inner knowing.

HOLY   The realisation of God consciousness.

INNER KNOWING   Understanding that comes from the higher aspect of yourself.

INTEGRITY   The experience of yourself intact, whole and in alignment with your inner truth.

KARMA   The tie to inner discord, created from the consequences of corruption created by you. Karma is released when resolve and harmony is reinstated within.

LIGHT   The realisation of the highest care in life.

LOVE   The essence of the creative life force in Holy Communion.

ONENESS   Realisation of the true state within where the Holy derives. Free from fear, karma and suffering.

POTENTIAL   The capacity for growth and expansion of life without limitation or restriction.

PRAYER Channelling Divine light into the matters of the heart.

PURPOSE The maturity of your light. Active service from self-realisation.

SENTIENT The perception of life through the feeling and sensory realm.

SHADOW Parts of you that have become hidden, distorted and separate from your truth.

SHAME A destructive and punitive force originating from the collective consciousness.

SHOWING The free expression of all of that you are.

SOVEREIGNTY Intact and complete within the self. In alignment to your truth and inner knowing.

SUPREME CONSCIOUSNESS The oneness state that surpasses all division of reality. The supreme self in realisation of the eternal light.

SURRENDER Allowing the sensitivity of your being to lead you. Guided by higher knowing without resistance.

TRUE SELF One's internal state free from discord and suffering.

TRUST To offer yourself with an open heart and hope.

TRUTH Seeing without the filters of distortion, resistance or manipulation. The untamed, permissible and correct state of being.

TYRANNY The misuse of power for self-gain and oppression.

VULNERABILITY   Accepting and showing your sensitivity and discomfort, without hiding behind masks.

WHOLENESS   The integrated self, where all parts of you are accepted. To live without borders.

WISDOM   The essential part of oneself derived from the understanding of truth.

WISH   To dream or imagine the potential in life.

Acknowledgements

I have come to know many beautiful souls who without, my journey could not have grown with love.

I thank my family, my mother and father for your strength and determination through such adversity, where your love and faith never failed us. To my sister and brothers for opening my heart with your consistent presence in my life. To Janet and Justus Klaar, for your warmth and support. To Jean Brodie, Shirley MacKenzie, Mark Halliday, Cláudia Gonçalves and Brian Anderson for your wisdom and care in my healing, I thank you for helping me realise the dream in me. To Paulo da Costa, you have given so much to strengthening my work, to Ana Clara Bárbara for your patience and love of beauty and to Gerard Lohan, Mark Grint and Hamish Campbell I thank you all for making the creative process of birthing this book so inspiring. To Maite Posada–Curros Buendía for your kindness, companionship and magical approach to exploring the mystery of life. To Kamila Sokolowski for the countless years of friendship and joy that has made my life so sweet.

And to my dear husband Nick, for your love and laughter that has held my heart and kept me earthed, to whom I am eternally grateful.

About the Author

Kefah has explored the practices and teachings of several traditions,– Islam, Sufism, Christianity, Anthroposophy, Theosophy, Buddhism and Shamanism. She has trained and studied in the healing practices of Energy Work, Reiki, Yoga, Counselling and Shamanism. She has worked extensively with individuals and groups, leading workshops, ceremonies and trainings in self-development, spiritual growth, healing and empowerment. Her work has developed as a writer and speaker sharing spiritual knowledge to help unlock higher potential. She currently lives and works in Edinburgh, Scotland.

Along her journey Kefah has taught dance, gardening, worked as a carer, gardener, support assistant and college tutor in arts/crafts.

Printed in Great Britain
by Amazon